**Better Homes and Gardens**®

# ASK THE EXPERTS

# CLEANING YOUR HOME

# 671 SECRETS THE PROS KNOW

*Ask the Experts: Cleaning Your Home*
**Editor:** Vicki Christian
**Contributing Writer:** Jana Finnegan
**Assistant Art Director:** Todd Emerson Hanson
**Contributing Graphic Designer:** Kim Jones
**Illustrator:** Mark Marturello
**Copy Chief:** Terri Fredrickson
**Publishing Operations Manager:** Karen Schirm
**Senior Editor, Asset and Information Manager:** Phillip Morgan
**Edit and Design Production Coordinator:** Mary Lee Gavin
**Editorial Assistant:** Kaye Chabot
**Book Production Managers:** Pam Kvitne, Marjorie J. Schenkelberg, Rick von Holdt, Mark Weaver
**Contributing Copy Editor:** Lorraine Ferrell
**Contributing Proofreaders:** Sue Fetters, Sherry Hames, Linda Wagner

**Meredith® Books**
**Executive Director, Editorial:** Gregory H. Kayko
**Executive Director, Design:** Matt Strelecki
**Executive Editor/Group Manager:** Denise Caringer
**Senior Associate Design Director:** Ken Carlson
**Marketing Product Manager:** Tyler Woods

**Publisher and Editor in Chief:** James D. Blume
**Editorial Director:** Linda Raglan Cunningham
**Executive Director, New Business Development:** Todd M. Davis
**Executive Director, Sales:** Ken Zagor
**Director, Operations:** George A. Susral
**Director, Production:** Douglas M. Johnston
**Director, Marketing:** Amy Nichols
**Business Director:** Jim Leonard

**Vice President and General Manager:** Douglas J. Guendel

*Better Homes and Gardens® Magazine*
**Editor in Chief:** Karol DeWulf Nickell
**Deputy Editor, Home Design:** Oma Blaise Ford

**Meredith Publishing Group**
**President:** Jack Griffin
**Executive Vice President:** Bob Mate

**Meredith Corporation**
**Chairman and Chief Executive Officer:** William T. Kerr
**President and Chief Operating Officer:** Stephen M. Lacy

**In Memoriam:** E.T. Meredith III (1933–2003)

All of us at Meredith® Books are dedicated to providing you with information and ideas to enhance your home. We welcome your comments and suggestions. Write to us at: Meredith Books, Home Decorating and Design Editorial Department, 1716 Locust St., Des Moines, IA 50309-3023.

If you would like to purchase any of our home decorating and design, cooking, crafts, gardening, or home improvement books, check wherever quality books are sold. Or visit us at: *bhgbooks.com.*

# CONTENTS

**Better Homes and Gardens®**

# Ask the Experts: Cleaning Your Home

## Introduction

You're in luck. The experts at *Better Homes and Gardens®* magazine have compiled all their best cleaning answers to help you get your home sparkling in no time.

For more than 80 years, *Better Homes and Gardens*® magazine has helped make life easier for millions of readers. Since 1922 there have been 996 issues of the magazine with more than 231,000 pages of information on everything from home decorating and cooking to cleaning and appliance care.

This handy book is a compilation of housecleaning tips and tricks to help you thoroughly and efficiently clean your home and give yourself more free time. That's time you can use to spend with your family and friends or pursue hobbies and adventures.

You will find specific advice from the experts at *Better Homes and Gardens*® magazine that you won't want to miss. You're busy, and your time is valuable—that's why this book is designed to help you eliminate housecleaning stress.

## You'll discover:

- **How to get motivated** and dig in
- **How to use tools of the trade**—some you can't live without, and many are staples in your kitchen that you already have on hand
- **How to get your family involved** and have fun cleaning
- **The best way to clean** wood floors, chandeliers, ceiling fans, and more
- **What makes bathtubs sparkle** and what keeps toilet bowls stain-free
- **How to clean green**—using natural products that are safe for kids and pets
- **A handy A–Z laundry guide,** with advice on getting out tough stains, from ketchup to grease and red wine
- **How to choose a cleaning service** if you decide you need one

O kay, admit it … cleaning your home is probably not at the top of your list of fun things to do. But now and then it becomes mandatory. And in the end you'll feel like a million bucks when the house is clean and sparkling again. If you've ever stood in the kitchen looking at crumbs on the counter, grit in the grout, and scum around the sink, you just might need some advice. This book brings you the knowledge and know-how to get housecleaning tasks done in a snap and get on with the really fun things in life.

## In this chapter you'll find:

- **Hints to motivate** you and the entire family
- **Handy tools** you can't clean without
- **Great cleansers** that really work
- **Money-saving ideas**
- **Special polishes** for unique surfaces
- **Daily and monthly routines** to help you get your cleaning chores organized
- **Fresh spring-cleaning ideas**

## Getting Started

Sometimes the anticipation of cleaning is far worse than actually rolling up your sleeves and getting the job done. Follow these simple suggestions to get motivated:

**Design A Plan.** Plan your serious housecleaning a day in advance, if possible, and you'll be ready to tackle almost any job.

**Limit Distractions.** Even the pros know that you can't get motivated to clean with a television on and your favorite snack on your lap. Turn off the phone too, if possible.

**Play Upbeat Music.** It's actually been proven that music will boost your adrenaline, so crank it up and see how much you can get done.

**Invest In Proper Cleaners** and gadgets to get the job done faster and easier.

**Tote Tools** in a rubber bucket or tray to keep them accessible. Stock your cleaning kit with plastic bags for trash, air fresheners to replace old and worn-out ones, and extra vacuum-cleaner bags.

**Clean Clockwise** in each room and make the circle only once.

**Make A List** of the chores you want to get done and don't quit until you're finished. Mark things off the list as you do them to motivate yourself.

**Inventory Products.** The day before you plan to clean, check your cleaning products to make sure you're well-prepared. Have old rags, sponges, scrub brushes, mops, and brooms ready to go. And don't forget to check the vacuum cleaner bag before getting started. There's nothing worse than having to run to the store because the vacuum bag has filled up, and you don't have more bags.

**Have Fun.** Don't look at cleaning as drudgery. Find ways to make it fun, such as asking a friend to help you clean your home and offering to reciprocate sometime. Promise yourself a special treat when you're done—whether it's a long bubble bath, a special dessert, that new book you've been wanting, or a manicure.

## Experts' Advice

### Choosing the Best Vacuum Cleaner

There are basically two types: an upright or a canister. An upright is much easier to use when simply vacuuming carpets. A canister is easier to use when you're vacuuming stairs or removing cobwebs in corners, but it's heavier. Either way you go, make sure to try it out in the store. Follow these steps to buy a vacuum cleaner you'll enjoy using:

- **Turn It On** to check the noise level.
- **Make Sure** it's got a long cord.
- **Get One** that's easy to maneuver.
- **If It Requires** a bag, buy one that has easy-to-find bags.
- **Choose Variable Speeds** if you have valuable rugs that need to be treated gently.
- **If You Buy an Upright,** make sure it comes with all the tools and attachments that you want and will use.

**Use String Mops.** They stand up to more dirt and liquid and can be bleached to look new again. When using these, change the water frequently to keep from swishing the same dirt around. Wring them out well, store them upright, and they'll be ready to use again.

**Make No-Cost** cleaning rags by cutting up old bath towels and T-shirts. Always machine wash cleaning rags after using them.

**Use Chamois Leather** for polishing windows after they've been washed with vinegar and water. Chamois is expensive but will last for years if you take care of it by following these suggestions:

- **Don't Use** liquid detergents or powdered cleaners to clean windows if you're using a chamois. The detergent will react with the natural oils in the chamois and destroy it. Instead, use denatured alcohol, white vinegar, or clear lukewarm water.
- **Wash Chamois** with warm water and soap flakes after each use; then rinse with clean water.
- **Don't Wring Out** the water; gently squeeze the cloth and shake it out flat.
- **Allow Chamois** to dry slowly away from direct heat and sunlight to keep the oils in the skin.

**Have Fun** with dusters. Who thought of making dusters in '70s disco colors? Well, it's a good thing someone did. They're fun, and they're dust magnets. So go ahead, grab a duster, crank up the music, and dance your way around the house—cleaning.

**Use Furniture Polish** sparingly, about once a month, to shine furniture. This will prevent a waxy buildup. The rest of the time, just dust furniture with a damp cloth and buff-dry.

**Use Beeswax Polish** to clean rough-textured, unpolished woods or to provide moisture if your wood furniture is dry. Rub the polish in and buff it to a shine with a soft cloth.

## Experts' Advice

### Cleaning on a Budget

If you're on a budget, here's good news: There are really only four cleaning products you need to clean everything around the house. You can save by purchasing these at the popular dollar stores springing up all over. Just be sure to check the expiration dates.

1. **Dishwashing Soap** cleans nearly everything from floors and showers to cabinet doors and knickknacks.

2. **Glass Cleaner** or vinegar works for anything that might show streaks—glass, mirrors, and appliances.

3. **Grease Cutter** is best for the really grimy jobs. Buy one with germ-killing power so it can do double duty to also disinfect.

4. **Dusting Spray** or cream polish for wood furniture is a good staple cleaning supply.

**Try Spray Lubricant** for greasing squeaky door hinges and getting paint off windows. Just spray it on the glass to loosen the paint and use a paint scraper to get the rest. Make sure your room is well-ventilated.

**Use Linen Tea Towels** in the kitchen because they're so absorbent. Use separate cloths to wash windows and spiff up silver. Keep another set handy to dry dishes and china. Wash and dry your hands on a third set so you don't spread germs and bacteria.

**Put Worn-Out Toothbrushes** in your cleaning supply carrier. They're just right for scrubbing dirty grout between tiles. Just mix one part bleach with one part water for the cleaning solution.

**Use Separate Gloves** for different jobs so you can keep bacteria from spreading. Buy them a size too big so they fit comfortably. Put hand cream on your hands, put cotton gloves on, and then rubber gloves. You've got a built-in spa treatment.

**Try Cotton Swabs** to clean inside and around cracks and crevices. They work well around the sink, in the track of your shower doors, and around the keys on the computer keyboard.

**Dip Cotton Balls** in a little rubbing alcohol to remove hairspray from bathroom surfaces like towel racks and mirrors. To freshen up a space, spray the cotton balls with your favorite scent (you could use the vanilla in your baking cupboard). Put them in an inconspicuous place such as under the seat in your car, in the linen closet, or under a piece of furniture.

# Must-Have Cleaning Products

Buying special cleaning products for specific cleaning tasks can make all the difference in the world in how quickly you finish the job. Often using what you have on hand in your kitchen might be the quickest route to take. To help you make that decision, check out these helpful tips:

**Try Dishwashing Liquid** to clean floors, walls, countertops, and appliances. Fill a bucket with hot water, add a capful or two of dishwashing liquid, and you'll be amazed at how many things you can clean around the house in a short amount of time.

**Use Scouring Powders** with caution. They work wonders on stains, but you can't use them on every surface. Look for the "scratch-free" versions to clean porcelain, stainless steel, fiberglass, natural marble, and glazed ceramic tile. But don't use them on plastic—they'll scratch the shine right off.

**Use Bleach To Brighten Surfaces.** It doesn't take much, but a bucket of warm water and 1/4 cup of bleach will work wonders on those white cupboards in the kitchen and bathroom.

**Use Nonabrasive Cream Cleansers** for delicate jobs. They work well on anything plastic in bathrooms and kitchens. They'll cut through grease without cutting out the shine.

**Wash Surfaces** with a solution of 1/4 cup baking soda and 2 quarts water. It cuts through grease and also keeps drains clean. Put a freshly opened box of baking soda in the refrigerator or freezer to keep food smelling fresh.

**Use Distilled Clear Vinegar** to remove lime scale caused by hard water. To clean windows, mix 1 part vinegar with 9 parts water. Spray the solution on windows and then rub off with newspaper so it won't leave streaks. Don't use this on plated surfaces as it can damage them.

**You Also Can Use** distilled clear vinegar on pet stains. Dilute the pet-stain spots with cold water or soda water. Mix 3 parts soda water with 1 part vinegar to clean the stain. Next, mix 1 ounce of ammonia with 10 ounces of water to rinse. This will remove any odor so pets will no longer recognize the territory as their own.

**Use Fabric Softener Sheets** for drying laundry and dusting miniblinds. Wipe them across your TV screens and computer monitors to repel dust. Wrap a sheet around the toilet paper holder before putting on a new roll. Then every time the paper is used, a fresh scent will spring into the air.

**Test Carpet Cleaner** spray on a hidden area of your carpet before using it. If it doesn't alter the color or texture of your carpet, use it to remove small marks. Really dirty carpets should be cleaned by a professional service.

# Cleaning and Polishing Special Surfaces

Metal surfaces, unfortunately, don't last forever. They can be easily scratched, wearing away the finish. Too much cleaning and polishing will eventually disfigure a metal object. So if a metal object is valuable to you, don't try to clean it yourself—take it to a jeweler. If you tackle the job yourself, here's how to do it without harming the surface:

**Wash Silver** in hot water and dishwashing liquid immediately after use and allow to dry. To remove scratches, buy jeweler's rouge from a jewelry store. Rub in the polish with a soft, dry cloth and use a special silver cleaning brush to get inside crevices. Rub lengthwise, not crosswise, or in circles.

**Clean Platinum** with a detergent-and-water solution (1 part detergent to 8 parts water) and dry. Dust precious gold lightly with a chamois cloth—ordinary cloths can scratch the metal. Clean low-karat gold with silver polish.

**Clean Chrome** by wiping it with a soft, damp cloth and polishing it with a dry one. Use a mild soap or detergent for sticky spills. Apple cider vinegar works well to polish chrome. Otherwise, a little paraffin on a damp cloth will clean up greasy deposits. Wipe on a thin film of silicone furniture polish to protect chrome trim and furnishings.

**Wash Stainless Steel** in hot, sudsy water. If the surface is really grimy, add ammonia to the water (2 tablespoons per quart). Clean sinks, countertops, and stove tops with borax instead of an abrasive cleaner that might scratch the surface.

**Don't Polish** lacquered brass—you might damage the surface. Just wash it occasionally in soapy water. To cut through dirt, use a solution of household ammonia and water. To keep it bright, apply a thin coat of paste wax to outdoor brass and lemon oil to indoor brass.

**Clean Copper Pans** with a commercial copper polish or make a homemade version from equal parts salt, vinegar, and flour. Treat really stubborn stains with a strong solution of household ammonia and water.

**Wash Bronze** with a solution of water and 10 percent acetic acid. Rinse well. Using wire brushes or harsh abrasives on bronze may damage the surface.

**Clean Pewter** naturally and safely by rubbing the surface with a cabbage leaf or the green part of a leek leaf. Rinse and dry. If your pewter is badly stained, try a little olive oil on fine steel wool and rub it carefully into the damaged area.

**Q.** How long do commercial cleaners last on the shelf? A year or two?

**A.** **Most Have a Long Shelf Life.** Just check the label for the expiration date.

**Scrub Lead Pieces** with turpentine or paint thinner. Soak a really dirty object in a solution of 1 part vinegar, 9 parts water, and 1 teaspoon of baking soda. This should dissolve the dirt and make it easier to clean. Rinse the piece in distilled water.

**Remove Rust** from wrought iron by rubbing it with steel wool dipped in kerosene. Soak small items in kerosene for a few hours and then rub them with steel wool. Polish with liquid wax. Wipe large wrought iron objects with cotton balls saturated with paint thinner. Wrought iron will rust if you use water for cleaning.

# Tackling Daily Cleaning Tasks

Keeping things neat and tidy really doesn't take much time and isn't a lot work. A few minutes spent putting things away each morning and evening will make your home look cleaner. Make it part of your daily routine to take care of the following chores:

# Every Morning

**Make The Beds** and feel as if you're using brand-new sheets every day. It also gives the house a tidy appearance when you come home.

**Pick Up Dirty Clothes** and put them in the hamper. (Better yet, have your family members pick up their own dirty clothes and put them in the hamper.) There's no sense tripping over sweat socks and discarded underwear all day.

**Put Clean Dishes Away** and do any dirty ones. A clean, empty sink does wonders for the looks of a kitchen and makes it seem as if a cleaning service has just been there.

 **Wipe Down Bathtubs,** showers, sinks, and counters in the bathroom for a fresh, clean look every day. The key is to do this in the morning when you're spending time there getting ready anyway.

 **Pour A Tablespoon** of lemon-scented cleaner in the toilet on your way out the door and leave it there all day for a fresh smelling bathroom.

# Every Evening

 **Load Dirty Dishes** in the dishwasher each evening and start the cycle. (Or do them by hand if you don't have a dishwasher.) Then you'll be all set for the next day.

 **Take The Trash Out** daily. That will help keep any leftovers from making their presence known by causing an odor. Before putting in a new trash bag, spray the inside of the pail with a disinfectant spray. It will kill germs and keep the kitchen smelling fresh.

 **Pick Up** items such as clothes, toys, and books, and take them to the room of the family member who owns them for that person to put away. Your whole house will look less cluttered in the morning.

**Use A Disinfectant Spray** on kitchen counters after cleaning up from dinner. Even when they look clean, countertops can host germs. Also wipe off the countertops, faucet, and faucet handles with disinfectant spray and a clean sponge soaked with hot, soapy water.

**Toss The Kitchen Sponge** in the top rack of the dishwasher (if you have one) at the end of the day. You'll have a clean, dry sponge after the cycle is over. You may have to replace sponges more often with this method, but you'll be assured that you're limiting the spread of germs and bacteria.

**Sterilize A Dry Sponge** by putting it in the microwave for 30 seconds at full power. To sterilize a wet sponge, put it in the microwave for 1 minute at full power.

**Q.**◆How can I clean a plasma TV so I don't ruin the surface? It was very expensive.

**A.**◆ **Clean the Flat Glass Screen** with a damp soft cloth. Abrasive cleaners or solvents can damage the screen.

 **Sweep The Kitchen Floor** at the end of the day so there won't be crumbs sticking to bare feet during the morning rush.

 **Wash, Dry, Fold,** and put away at least one load of laundry every day. By keeping up with laundry regularly, you won't have a daunting mountain of it waiting for you on weekends.

 **Tidy Up Coffee Tables** and end tables in areas that guests can see, just in case unannounced visitors stop by.

# Every Week

Maintain a weekly cleaning routine to get all your tasks done during the weekdays and keep your weekends free. Don't get discouraged if you miss a day. Split the missed tasks between the next two cleaning days or do them the next week.

 **The Night Before Trash Day—Take Just 10 Minutes.** Walk through the house and gather all the trash the night before trash day. There's nothing worse than waking up to the sound of the trash pickup truck gathering everyone's garbage except yours.

## Experts' Advice

# Establish Weekly Cleaning Routines

**Monday—30 Minutes**
- Do a load of laundry while you're getting ready in the morning.
- Empty the trash.
- Vacuum all the carpets.
- Sweep off the front steps and the deck.

**Tuesday—40 Minutes**
- Wash the area rugs.
- Mop the kitchen and bathroom floors.
- Clean the mirrors and wash down the doors and doorknobs.
- Feather-dust furniture.

**Wednesday—30 Minutes**
- Clean out the refrigerator.
- Write out a grocery list and plan weekly menus.
- Balance your checkbook before going shopping.

**Thursday—60 Minutes**
- Do all the grocery shopping for the week in one trip.
- Run errands for the week. Don't forget to drop off your dry cleaning, stop by the post office, get birthday gifts that you might need for the week, and send anniversary and birthday cards to family and friends.

**Friday—30 Minutes**
- Clean the laundry/mudroom.
- Change the sheets while making the beds.

# Ideas for Spring and Deep Cleaning

Spring and deep cleaning are probably the hardest chores to tackle. Start early in the morning when your energy is high. Wear cast-off clothes, so you won't worry about dirt or stains. Promise yourself a special treat or reward at the end of your cleaning session.

# Spring and Deep Cleaning Checklist

Consider this your checklist for a day of spring cleaning to make the day go by in a snap. Or complete one task per day for several weeks, and your spring cleaning will get done over time instead of consuming an entire day.

- ❏ **Transfer Out-of-Season Clothing** to an unused closet. Donate to charity clothing you haven't worn for two years. Ask for a receipt—you may be able to deduct it from your taxes.

- ❏ **Strip the Beds.** Wash blankets, comforters, and quilts—dust mites thrive there. Clean the bedding and vacuum the mattress.

- ❏ **Defrost the Refrigerator** and freezer (if yours aren't frost-free) and use up frozen goods that have been hanging around a while.

- ❏ **Move Heavy Furniture** and clean behind and under it. You may find enough change around the house to indulge in a latte later in the day to reward your cleaning efforts.

- ❏ **Shampoo or Professionally Clean Carpets,** upholstered furniture, and drapes.

- ❏ **Clean Out the Chimney** or have it done professionally. You'll lower your risk of fire if you do this each season.

- ❏ **Check the Furnace** and air conditioning prior to the respective seasons that you use them.

- ❏ **Oil Sliding Door Tracks** to keep them working properly.

- ❏ **Clean Screens** and storm doors on a sunny, warm day.

# Dining and Living Room Lowdown

**T**he dining room and living room may be the most formal rooms in a home and the ones guests see most often. Take your time to clean them carefully, especially if you have heirlooms, antique furnishings, and expensive window coverings. In this chapter the experts at *Better Homes and Gardens*® magazine bring you handy tips for keeping these rooms tidy with minimum effort. You'll see how to do the following:

- **Clean wood** and glass furniture
- **Care for antiques** and valuable furnishings
- **Spiff up soiled fabrics** on window coverings and furniture
- **Make chandeliers sparkle**
- **Keep fireplaces clean** and safe
- **Add shine** to silk and live plants

## Dusting ABCs

Dust your furniture as often as you like, but use furniture polish or wax just once or twice yearly to reduce the risk of buildup. Here are a few other dusting tips:

**Dust With A Damp Cloth.** Rinse it out occasionally in clean water and wring it out as you go. Toss dirty dusting cloths in the washer.

**Vacuum Furniture,** baseboards, and moldings with a soft brush attachment. Use care to avoid scratching delicate surfaces.

**Try Homemade Polish.** Mix 1/2 cup white vinegar, 1/2 cup turpentine, and 1/2 cup boiled linseed oil. (Add 3 teaspoons flavored extract from your kitchen cupboard for fragrance.) You also can clean wood furniture with a mixture of 1 part olive oil and 1 part lemon oil. Apply either mixture with a soft, damp cloth and polish with another dry one.

**Remove Polish Buildup** by buffing furniture with a combined mixture of 1 part vinegar and 1 part water on a clean rag.

**Eliminate Water Rings** by applying regular mayonnaise to the spots. Leave on for several hours or overnight. Wipe the spots with a clean, soft cloth the next day.

# Caring for Antiques

Furniture polish doesn't penetrate the surface and feed the wood as you might think. It merely fills the fine scratches and makes it easier to dust the next time. To clean and care for your antiques and collectibles more thoroughly, try these tips:

**Clean Corners** and crevices carefully with a soft toothbrush.

**Dust Carved Furniture** with feather or lamb's-wool dusters. These get into the crevices well and keep them dust free.

**Clean Up Alcohol Spills** on wood furniture by immediately wiping up the excess liquid and then rubbing the area with your hand. The oil in your hand will help restore some of the oil taken out of the wood by the alcohol.

**Get A Quick Wax** by rubbing wood surfaces with a new sheet of wax paper and then buffing them with a soft cloth.

**Smooth Sticky Drawer** runners by rubbing them with a white candle or sprinkling them with talcum powder.

**Straighten Up** coffee tables at the end of each day—your room will look cleaner and fresher every morning when you wake up.

**Rub Glass Tabletops** with lemon juice or vinegar and dry them with paper towels. Buff them with newspaper for a streak-free shine.

**Remove Stains** on marble furniture by applying a paste of chalk dust mixed with acetone (available at chemical supply stores). Then cover the area with plastic wrap and seal it with masking tape. Let it set a few hours and wipe with a moist cloth. If the surface looks dull, wet it with water, sprinkle it with marble-polishing powder, and rub it with a thick soft cloth.

**Wipe Rush,** sea-grass, or twisted fibers with a damp cloth only when necessary.

**Clean Metal Furniture** occasionally with warm, sudsy water.

**Brush Or Vacuum** wicker and bamboo regularly to keep dust from clinging. Use sudsy water and borax with a soft brush to get into the small cracks and crevices.

**Use Saddle Soap** and as little water as possible to clean leather furniture. Let it dry and buff it with a soft cloth.

## Experts' Advice

### Care of Gilded Pieces

- **Gently Dust** pieces with a feather duster. Or clean them with a soft cloth lightly dipped in warm turpentine or paint thinner. (Warm these solvents by standing the bottle in warm water.)

- **Don't Use Water** on gilded pieces—it may damage the surface.

- **Avoid Handling** these pieces as much as possible. Keep them out of direct heat and sunlight to help preserve their beauty.

# Tips on Cleaning Furniture and Window Coverings

Experts agree that the best way to keep fine fabrics on upholstered furniture and draperies in top condition is to vacuum them regularly. Vacuuming prevents surface dirt, dust, animal dander, and food from settling into the fabric and creating long-term damage. With regular vacuuming, your fabrics will keep their original vibrant colors and textures for years. Here are a few more tips:

**Spot-Check** furniture cushions for small items like toys, buttons, keys, or coins before you vacuum as these can block and potentially damage the vacuum hose.

**Deep-Clean** chairs and seats occasionally before they look dirty. Rinse thoroughly after you've deep-cleaned them. Furnishings rapidly show stains again if you don't properly remove all the detergent or cleaner.

**Don't Soak Cushions** you're cleaning—foam and feathers can break down or lump together if they get too wet.

**Use Silicone Sprays** on upholstered furniture to prevent dirt buildup and stains. Be sure to follow the instructions on the product label.

**Iron Cotton** and linen slipcovers by pressing them on the wrong side while they're still damp. Put covers back immediately so they'll dry to their original shape.

**Remove Dust** and dirt from drapes and curtains by vacuuming. Use the upholstery attachments because brush attachments can cause damage to the fabric.

**Take Large Drapes** to a self-service laundry that has larger capacity machines or have them professionally cleaned and treated.

**Remove Hooks** or weights from drapes before washing so the fabric won't be damaged.

**Wash Lined Drapes** following the washing instructions for the weakest fiber listed in the blend of fabric.

**Stretch Cotton Drapes** gently before hanging so they'll hang correctly when they dry.

**Soak Lace Curtains** in warm, sudsy water to clean them. Don't rub, twist, or wring; just move the fabric gently around in the water. Lay flat to dry.

## Experts' Advice

### Whitening Lace Curtains

If your white curtains have become dingy and gray, here are a few tips to lighten them:

- **Try Whitening** nylon curtains with a commercial product made for whitening lingerie, available at home stores. Rinse the curtains well after using the product as directed.

- **Brighten Cotton Curtains** by first soaking them in cold water and then using an oxy-clean detergent.

- **Rehang Nylon** and cotton curtains while slightly damp to allow creases to smooth out naturally to save ironing time.

# Cleaning Ceilings and Walls

The ceilings and walls in your dining room and living room may have special paints, papers, fabrics, or tiles that require special care. In that case the only cleaning necessary on a regular basis is dusting. Here are a few tricks from the experts of *Better Homes and Gardens*® to keep these surfaces spotless:

**Dust The Ceiling** with the dusting attachment fitted to your vacuum hose, a long-handled feather duster, or a flexible broom head. You also can use a clean dust cloth tied over the head of a broom.

 **Brush Nonwashable Wallpapers** occasionally with a soft brush, a handheld vacuum, or the head of a broom covered with a dust cloth.

 **Clean Washable Wall Coverings** with an all-purpose cleaner. Be sure to rinse thoroughly to avoid leaving a film on the wallpaper.

 **Wipe Down Wall Murals** with a clean damp sponge only if they're made of heavy-duty poster paper. Use soft brushing movements since scrubbing can cause surface damage. Call the manufacturer to determine the mural's composition if you're unsure.

 **Use An Old Toothbrush** to clean embossed wallcoverings.

 **Spray Decorative Moldings** with a general cleaning solution. Use a paintbrush or an old toothbrush to remove dirt in the crevices. Then spray the area with plain water and dry it with a soft terry cloth towel.

 **Clean Glass** over precious artwork with a soft cloth sprayed with rubbing alcohol.

# Fireplace Cleanup

With these tips from the *Better Homes and Gardens*® experts, your family can safely enjoy a fire in the fireplace:

**Hire A Professional** chimney sweep at the beginning of each heating season to make sure the chimney is in good working order.

**Remove Remaining Ashes** or other debris with a flat fireplace shovel. To cut down on the dust, spread some used, wet coffee grounds on the ashes first and then shovel them. Place them in a bucket for easy removal and disposal.

**Use A Shop Vacuum** with a filter bag to remove remaining ashes or debris.

**Remove Soot** and fire stains from the firebox with soapy water. For tough-to-remove stains, allow a liberal amount of solution to stay on the surface for 30 minutes and scrub surfaces with a stiff wire brush.

**Use Spray Lubricant** to wipe soot away from the metal fire surround on the fireplace. The oily film will help make cleaning the surround even easier next time.

**Try Oven Cleaner** to clean glass fireplace doors. Use a damp cloth to apply a little to the cooled glass window and then rinse well with water.

**Q.** When we use our wood-burning fireplace, I notice dust. What wood should I burn that won't create so much dust?

**A.** **To Reduce Soot and Dust,** use clean-burning woods like oak, ash, hickory, and other hardwoods. They are not as messy as softer woods, so you won't have to clean so often.

## Sparkle Up Chandeliers and Sconces

There's nothing like enlivening a room with the fragments of light reflected from a chandelier or wall sconce onto the ceiling, walls, and floor. Chandeliers, wall sconces, and any other wall fixtures can be cleaned easily if you follow these tips:

**Dust Chandeliers** and light fixtures each time you clean a room for easy maintenance.

**Wear Cotton Gloves** to clean your chandeliers. That makes it easy to dip your hands in an ammonia-and-water solution. Then squeeze out the excess solution and wipe the crystals clean. Wear rubber gloves under the cotton gloves to protect your hands.

**Clean Chandeliers** and light fixtures in place with special spray cleaners that allow you to let them "drip dry." First turn off the electricity.

# Cleaning Decorative Moldings

The nooks and crannies of decorative moldings are easier to clean than you may think. Here are a few tricks to try:

**Remove The Dust** in the nooks and crannies of moldings with the brush attachment or crevice tool of a vacuum cleaner.

**Wash Grimy Moldings** with a mixture of 1 cup ammonia, 1/2 cup white vinegar, and 1/4 cup baking soda in 1 gallon of warm water. Put the mixture in a spray bottle and squirt it directly into dusty corners and crevices. Wipe dry with a soft cloth.

**Don't Wash** plaster moldings that are badly chipped and cracked because that may cause further damage. Wipe them clean with a soft cloth.

# Bright Ideas for Lampshades

Here are a few simple solutions for keeping lamps and shades clean and dust free:

**Start Cleaning** a lamp by removing the shade. Dust or vacuum the shade and then wipe the bulb with a dry cloth.

**Wash Glass** or plastic globes and reflectors in warm sudsy water. Rinse and dry carefully. Or, wipe them with a chamois cloth dampened with rubbing alcohol or paint thinner. Then buff them with a lint-free cloth.

**Clean Glass Bases** with a damp cloth wrung out in clear or sudsy water. Wipe marble and alabaster bases with a damp cloth. Clean porcelain, glazed stoneware, and china bases with a cloth wrung out in mild sudsy water. Rinse and wipe dry with a paper towel or lint-free cloth.

**Dust Lacquered Bases** occasionally. Too-frequent dusting may damage the surface.

**Vacuum Lampshades** lightly once yearly to remove dust. Don't plunge lampshades into water unless you know that treatment to be safe.

**Use A Feather Duste**r on metal or paper shades.

**Dry-Clean Silk Lampshades** professionally before they begin to look dirty.

# Are You Floored?

A wood floor, terrazzo floor, and even carpet can attract dust and look as if it's dirty when it's not. Keep floors looking their best with these tips:

**Clean Hardwood Floors** by damp-mopping a small area at a time using warm water and then wiping the surface dry.

**Damp-Mop Painted Floors** with a mild detergent solution, using as little water as possible.

**Wax Or Polish Painted Floors** to make them easy to clean.

**Wash Glossy Enamel Floors** with hot water to cut through the dirt.

**Wash Waterproof Varnished Floors** with warm, soapy water.

**Flip Area Rugs** around periodically so all areas will wear evenly, and soiling will be evenly distributed over the surface.

**Remove Stains** from rugs and carpeting as soon as possible.

**Pour Salt** on a fresh liquid spill and let it set for an hour. Vacuum or blot the salt with a paper towel. Change towels as they become saturated.

**Scrape Up Solid Spills** on rugs and carpeting with the back of a knife. Rubbing these spills will only send them farther into the floor covering. If the spill leaves a mark, apply carpet stain remover and follow label directions. For tough stains, call the professionals.

# Clean Those Greens

Live, artificial, or silk plants can beautify any home. Keeping the leaves and stems clean is essential to the health of live plants. Artificial trees, silk plants, and silk flowers will benefit from a good cleaning every 3–6 months. *Better Homes and Gardens*® experts offer these suggestions:

**Test Artificial Leaves** for water safety. Rinse a leaf in an inconspicuous area. Shake it out and check it after a few minutes to see if the leaf is shiny again.

**Check The Filler** in the pot of silk and artificial plants to make sure it can withstand a wet cleaning. Some plants are set in paper, and you'll end up with a mess. You can proceed if the plant is set in a foam base.

**Protect Brass** and copper pots during cleaning with a trash bag tied up at the base of the plant.

**Wash Plants** outside on a patio or driveway. Using a spray nozzle on the hose, spray plants thoroughly, and then shake them lightly to remove most of the water. Allow plants to dry for a few hours in the sun.

**"Dry-Clean"** artificial and silk plants by adding 1 cup of salt to a plastic grocery store bag. Turn your plants or flowers top first into the bag and tie the handles around the stem. Shake the bag for two minutes and your plants will be dust free.

**A Good Plant Cleaner** contains 2 parts water and 1 part vinegar in a spray bottle. Spray the mixture on the leaves and wipe them dry with a cotton-gloved hand. (Wearing the glove to dry them makes the process faster and keeps your cleaning rags from becoming stained.)

# Liven Up Living Plants

Handling your live plants with care will bring you years of enjoyment and beauty. Here are a few tips to keep the "greens" clean:

**Clean Indoor Plants** with an occasional "shower" of clear or light soapy water. This will help your plants grow larger and live longer. Rinse off soapy water so you don't clog the leaf pores. Do this outdoors on a "gray" day instead of in direct sunlight. Cleaning three to four times per year is usually a good cleaning routine for live plants.

**Wear Cotton Gloves** to clean live plants. Use one hand as a "wiper" and the other as a "dryer." Wipe from the stem of the leaf to the tip on both the top and the bottom. Use a moist glove to apply gentle pressure to remove dust from the surface of the leaf. Then dry the leaf with the dry glove before moving on.

**Don't Use** commercial leaf-shine products. These may clog the pores of the leaves and inhibit plant respiration. These products also may limit the plant's ability to absorb light.

**Use The Inside** of a banana peel to dust live plant leaves. You'll love the shine, and they'll love the nutrients.

# Kitchen Magic

That magic in your kitchen isn't just the food that's prepared, or the long conversations during dinnertime with the whole family sitting around the table. Part of the magic in this gathering place is finding a way for it to stay self-cleaning. You'll love some of the ideas that our experts have for doing just that. It'll give you a break from extra work and give you more time to spend doing other things you love.

The experts at *Better Homes and Gardens®* magazine have found hints to help your kitchen sparkle and stay that way. In the next pages you'll learn:

- **Which germs love kitchens** and how to deal with them quickly
- **How to keep sponges and cutting boards clean** and sanitary for constant use
- **Proper food storage techniques** that world-renowned chefs use
- **Ways to keep food stains** from ruining your dinnerware and utensils
- **Simple cleaning techniques** for all your appliances
- **How to keep your pans** revitalized and your bakeware in tip-top shape

## Guard Against Bacteria and Germs

Bacteria and germs love food and beverages just as much as you do. The kitchen is their target because it gives them a playground of places to live, grow, and breed. Killing germs in trash cans, on countertops, and elsewhere will keep your kitchen spotless and your family healthier. In this chapter you'll discover advice for eliminating germs and pests.

**Bacteria And Germs** are spread most often by hands—through hand-to-hand contact or hand-to-surface-to-hand contact. Here are a few tidbits of information on these invisible invaders. They:

- **May Enter** the body through the eyes, the nose, the mouth, and scratches on the skin.
- **Can Live** on dry surfaces for several hours and on moist surfaces for a few days. (So keep counters wiped off and dry.)
- **Are Hardy.** Salmonella can withstand freezing and survive 24 hours on dry surfaces.
- **Love Kitchen Dishcloths.** An average kitchen dishcloth can have 4 billion germs living on it at any given time.
- **Can Cause Food Poisoning,** intestinal illnesses, skin infections, and commonly transmitted diseases. Use antibacterial solutions to wash your hands often when cooking and cleaning.

**Flies** love food and aren't fussy about where they land and what they touch. They carry around 2 million bacteria on their tiny bodies, hatch eggs in 24 hours, and can rapidly spread bacteria that can cause cholera, dysentery, diarrhea, and typhoid. Do these things during fly season:

- **Don't Leave Food Out**, uncovered, in the kitchen. Make sure dirty dishes aren't piled in the sink.
- **Buy Trash Cans** for the kitchen with tight-fitting lids to keep flies from enjoying a feast.
- **Use Disinfectant** on all surfaces in the kitchen. Do this prior to cooking and as you clean up.

**Roaches And Beetles** can turn into a real problem if they aren't carefully controlled. Unfortunately, you may bring these food pests home in food products that were actually infested at the store. If you leave the package open at home, insects can spread to other food. Stop them in their tracks and limit your risk of pest infestation through these expert recommendations:

- **Store Food** in containers that act as barriers to pests. Plastic, glass, and metal containers with lids that fit tight will keep food safe.
- **Don't Overstock** your pantry. Use food products in a short period of time.
- **Clean Up Spills** immediately and be sure to get in the cracks, crevices, and corners where roaches and beetles feast at night.

**Ants** are a dual problem. Some ants love sweet foods and others enjoy grease. Here are your best bets for avoiding them visiting you:

- **Clean Up Spills** and food scraps left on the sink, counter, table, and floor.
- **Keep Fruits** and vegetables in the refrigerator.
- **Wash And Dry Countertops** immediately after cooking and serving dinner.
- **Caulk Around Doors** and windows where the intruders may be coming in.

# Clean These Items Often

Dirt, germs, and unseen bacteria are abundant in the kitchen. From time to time you might want to clean kitchen items that you don't even know need cleaning. Rest assured that if you tackle them promptly, you'll be healthier and happier just knowing your kitchen is clean.

**Choose Waffle-Weave** cotton cloths as the top kitchen-cleaning tools. Use one to wipe off dirty surfaces and another to wash dishes. Keeping the towels separated by colors means you'll always use the same cloth for the same task.

**Use Two Chopping Boards** in the kitchen —one for vegetables and one for raw meat. Germs can live several hours on chopping boards. Scrub them in hot soapy water and rinse in the hottest water possible before allowing them to air-dry.

**Use Paper Towels** to wipe up meat juices and blood from countertops instead of using dishcloths or rags. Throw the towels away immediately and clean off the counter with a disinfecting spray and wipe it dry.

**Place Sink Stoppers** in the basket of your dishwasher when you run it. They'll look brand new and be germ-free most of the time.

**Soak Sponges** in salt water occasionally to freshen them. Rinse them out with clear water. Kill any remaining bacteria by putting sponges in the microwave on high for 1 minute. Be careful—they'll be hot. You also can put sponges in a basket on the top rack of your dishwasher when you run it. You might have to replace them more often, but you'll have a clean sponge each time.

**Add A Cup Of Vinegar** to a pail of mop water. It cleans dirt and grime and gives floors a shine.

# Clean Counters, Sinks, and Chrome Easily

**Follow The Manufacturer's Recommendations** when cleaning kitchen counters. For a general cleaner, mix equal parts water and lemon juice in a spray bottle. Add a teaspoon of salt, and shake well.

**Use Baking Soda** to remove coffee stains from countertops. Use the soda as a cleanser to buff out stains with a damp cloth.

**Eliminate Stubborn Water Spots** in and around your kitchen sink with rubbing alcohol. Rinse with white vinegar or club soda afterward. Buff to a shine with a soft cloth or paper towel.

**Restore Whiteness** to ceramic sinks by adding a cup of bleach to a sink of water. Leave the water for half an hour and then rinse thoroughly.

**Remove Lime Scale** from the kitchen tap with fresh lemon juice. Cut a fresh lemon in half and rub over the surface. Allow it to work for a few minutes and then rinse clean. Repeat again if your tap is heavily scaled.

**Clean Lime Scale** from chrome and stainless steel with distilled clear vinegar. Rub the vinegar on with a paper towel, let stand for a few hours, and then rinse with clear water. It'll also remove watermarks from sinks and drainers. Just wipe dry with paper towels when you're through.

**Use Lighter Fluid To Remove Rust Marks** in a stainless-steel sink. (But, be careful: It's highly flammable.) Use lemon juice to get rid of rust stains on porcelain sinks.

# Store Food Successfully

If you have food-storage phobia, see these tips and tricks from the *Better Homes and Gardens®* experts to keep your food safe to eat and stored properly for future meals:

**Don't Overstock Your Pantry.** Instead, restock it often so you limit the risk of pests enjoying the food before you do.

**Store Dried Foods** in heavy plastic or glass containers with tight-fitting lids. Stackable storage containers are even better. You'll keep your cupboards looking neat and tidy while you keep your food safe.

**Discard Old Fruits And Vegetables.** The aging fruit will attract fruit flies, while spoiling vegetables will cause still-fresh veggies to spoil also.

**Be Aware Of Potentially Hazardous Foods.** The FDA identifies the following foods as potentially hazardous—sometimes causing foodborne illnesses. Take special care storing milk and milk products, shell eggs, meats, poultry, fish, shellfish, baked or boiled potatoes, tofu or other soy-protein foods, garlic-in-oil mixtures, fruits and vegetables, raw seeds and sprouts, sliced melons, and synthetic ingredients such as soy protein.

## Experts' Advice

# Watch Cooking and Storing Times and Temperatures

Safe food storage also includes holding foods at a proper temperature while serving them, cooking them to a desired temperature, cooling hot foods quickly, and storing leftovers. Here are a few tips:

- **The Danger Zone** for temperature is between 41° F and 140° F. Keep foods colder than 41° F or warmer than 140° F, even on your holiday buffet.

- **Safe Cooking Temperatures** are needed for many foods. Cook poultry, stuffing, and stuffed meat to 165° F; ground meats to 155° F; injected meats to 155° F; pork, beef, veal and lamb to 145° F; fish and fresh shell eggs to 145° F; and any potentially hazardous food cooked in the microwave to 165° F for at least two minutes.

- **Cool Hot Foods Quickly** to prevent bacterial growth. Do as famous chefs do and put hot soups, stews, and gravies in a container in an ice bath and give them a stir now and then. The quicker they get into the refrigerator the better.

- **Store Leftover Food** either in tightly wrapped plastic or in plastic containers with tight-fitting lids to avoid leaks. Use the "first in, first out" (FIFO) method that chefs use so leftovers won't stay in the refrigerator too long and spoil.

## Experts' Advice

### Store It in Order

To keep food items safe and at less risk of contamination, it's best to **store them in the following order, from the top down**:

1. **Cooked and Ready-to-Eat** food
   (like packaged yogurts, puddings, cakes, and pies)

2. **Whole Fish**

3. **Whole Meat**

4. **Ground Meat**

5. **Poultry**

**TIP 150**

**Are You In Doubt** about the freshness of a certain food? Then throw it out. That's the safest precaution to help prevent foodborne illnesses.

**TIP 151**

**Be Sure To Label** leftovers (whether you put them in a container or wrap them with foil or plastic wrap) with the contents and the date. This way you won't end up with "mystery" leftovers.

# Stamp Out Food Stains and Odors

Use these handy hints to help avoid unpleasant stains and odors:

**Eliminate Odors** on plastic utensils by soaking them overnight in warm water with ¼ teaspoon dry mustard.

**Remove Hard-Water Buildup** from ice cube trays by soaking them in full-strength vinegar for several hours.

**Eliminate Egg Stains** from silver by rubbing the stains gently with salt before thoroughly washing them.

**Remove Rust On Knives** by sticking the blade in an onion, moving it back and forth a few times, and leaving it in the onion for a few hours. The acid in the onion juice will eat away the rust.

**Brighten Dingy Aluminum Utensils** by mixing 2 quarts of water with 8 tablespoons of vinegar or cream of tartar. Boil utensils for 10 minutes and then rinse well. Scour any remaining stains with #0000 steel-wool and rinse again.

# Hot Talk About Stoves

Appliances might be the last things on your list to clean because they don't get that dirty most of the time. And, about the time you notice they do need to be cleaned, you're just about to use them again. Since most appliances get used every day for something as important as food storage or preparation, it's important to keep them clean. A quick cleanup now and then will save you a long, difficult cleaning later. To care for your stove, check out these hot tips:

**Wipe Up Spatters** on the stove top while they're still warm—before they're burned on and harder to remove. Keep a damp cloth handy while you work so you can clean up as you go along.

**Clean Removable Parts** on the stove top monthly or after a major cooking. That way, you won't have burnt-on spatters to clean up later. Usually hot soapy water and a clean dishcloth work best.

**Clean Drip Trays And Drip Pans** by soaking a cloth in ammonia and laying it over the tray or pan. Let it soak overnight and wash it off the next day.

**Shine Your Stove Top** with rubbing alcohol on a paper towel or cloth for a streak-free surface.

**Use Cleaning Products** recommended by the manufacturer for special stove tops such as those made of halogen or ceramic tile. Clean up spills fast to prevent surface damage.

**Check Manufacturer's Instructions** on how to clean up after self-cleaning ovens. Usually, when cleaning is done, a light gray ash remains on the oven floor. Just wipe it up with a clean sponge.

**Clean Brown Stains** from oven windows with a paste of baking soda and water. Just coat the window with the paste and let it set for 20 minutes. You should be able to scour off the stain.

**Protect With Aluminum Foil.** Once you've got your oven clean, cover the bottom with a sheet of aluminum foil to catch any boil-over mess. Then you can just throw the foil away when it gets dirty.

# Master the Microwave

**Put A Dish** of hot water in the microwave for easy cleanup. Add a slice of lemon and boil the water for about 2 minutes until steam is produced. Keep the door closed another 5 minutes and then wipe the interior with a damp cloth.

 **Shine The Outside** of the microwave with a cloth dipped in hot, soapy water. Follow up with window cleaner on the window and over the keypad.

 **Vacuum Dusty Vents** now and then with a soft-brush attachment from the vacuum cleaner.

 **Clean The White Interior** of the microwave with a paste of baking soda and water. Rinse well after cleaning. Harsh abrasives may scratch the interior, so avoid them.

 **Put Microwave Carousel Trays** in the dishwasher for easy cleanup. Or cover them with wax wrap. If you replace the wrap now and then, you won't have to clean carousels very often.

 **Keep Your Microwave Clean** by covering plates and dishes with a lid, or even a paper towel when heating foods. It helps prevent food splatters when you're cooking.

# Refresh Your Refrigerator

**Clean Your Refrigerator** while you're in the kitchen making a meal. Use a cloth with baking soda and warm water to wipe down bottles, jars, and containers.

**Wipe Up Sticky Spills** right away. If you leave them, they'll be harder to clean up and could begin to smell or develop mold.

**Clean Automatic-Defrosting** refrigerators about three times a year. Once or twice a year, clean the condenser coils under, behind, or on top of the refrigerator. Pry off the grille and vacuum with a crevice tool. Remove the drain pan at the bottom, and wash it in soapy water.

**Clean White Appliances** with a mixture of 6 cups water, ⅓ cup bleach, and ⅓ cup baking soda. This will prevent ugly yellowing. After cleaning, rinse well with clear water. Then rinse off with a vinegar-water mixture. Caution: Never mix vinegar with bleach. Never use this solution on stainless-steel appliances.

**Remove Finger Marks** on stainless steel by buffing them out with a small amount of baby oil on a clean cloth. Then rinse off with a cloth dampened with club soda.

**Enjoy A Peppermint Scent** by soaking a cotton ball in peppermint extract and placing it in the refrigerator.

**Use Plastic Place Mats** to line a shelf or two in your refrigerator. That way, if anything spills, cleanup is quicker and easier because it's confined to one mat instead of the entire shelf.

# Defrost the Freezer

- **Defrost The Freezer** regularly. This will keep it operating more efficiently. As you defrost move the contents around and organize them so you'll know what you need to use first.

- **Open The Door** to the freezer as little as possible to keep it from icing up and producing frost. To be really organized post a list of the freezer's contents on the outside of the freezer door and mark off foods as you use them. It saves you standing with the door open, rummaging through the food.

- **Melt Ice Quickly.** For a quick-and-easy ice melt in the freezer, place open bowls of hot water on towels on the shelves to melt the ice with the steam. Place a sheet pan on the bottom of the freezer to catch the drips. (Change bowls of hot water when they become cool.)

- **Clean Up The Rest** of the freezer sections while the freezer is defrosting. Wash out the drawers and dry them well. Then clean up the drip pan if your freezer has one.

- **Eliminate Dust Bunnies** by dusting an upright freezer with the brush end of your car's ice scraper. It also works well on the coils on the back of the freezer.

- **Reduce Odors** by placing an open loaf of fresh bread in the freezer and leaving it a few days. It soaks up any lingering smells.

# Remember Small Appliances

**Unplug Electrical Appliances** from the wall before cleaning. Never immerse them in water.

**Clean Your Toaster** by opening the removable plate on the bottom of the toaster and giving it a gentle shake over the trash can. Wipe the exterior with a damp cloth for an extra shine.

**Use Acetone-Soaked Cotton Balls** or cloths to clean up melted plastic on your toaster. Nail polish remover works well too.

**Loosen Lime Scale** deposits from tea kettles by adding two denture cleaning tablets to a kettle full of water. Let it set overnight. In the morning, wipe away the deposits with paper towels and then rinse well.

**Dissolve Mineral Deposits** from a coffeemaker by running a carafe filled with a solution of half white vinegar and half water through it occasionally. Follow up by running through a carafe of plain water. You can use a toothpick to clean residue from the drip tube.

**Prevent Mineral Deposits** in your drip coffeemaker by putting a marble or a piece of loofah sponge inside it. Mineral deposits will accumulate there rather than on the element.

**Clean Electric Can Openers** by soaking an old toothbrush in vinegar. Then hold it under the blade/wheel. Turn on the machine and the toothbrush will remove any dirt or residue.

# Pamper Your China, Porcelain, Plastic, and Glass

**Promptly Rinse China** used for egg or milk dishes with cold water and then wash.

 **Remove Tea And Coffee Stains** on cups or mugs by rubbing with a wet cloth dipped in dry baking soda or a salt-and-water paste.

 **Wash Old China** by hand in warm, not hot, water. If you wash china or glazed finishes in very hot water, tiny cracks can appear. Don't soak pieces with gold glazes or trim; the water may lift the glaze off. Don't put china in your dishwasher.

 **Food Stains On Plastic** can usually be removed with a mild solution of chlorine bleach and water.

 **Remove Tomato And Tea Stains** on plastic with bleach and hot water. Allow the plastic to soak for a few minutes and then rinse thoroughly.

 **Avoid Extreme Temperatures** with all glassware. For example, putting cold glasses into very hot water may cause them to break.

 **If You're In Doubt** whether to put china or other fragile pieces in the dishwasher, don't. In general, china is susceptible to heat and sunlight.

 **Safely Store China** by stacking paper plates, doilies, or paper towels between the pieces. Keep the stacks short so the weight won't cause damage.

# Caring for Knives

For the at-home chef, keeping knives clean and sharp will result in a lifetime of cooking pleasure. Whether you have expensive or inexpensive knives, care for them the same. Cleaning, storing, and sharpening knives properly will keep them in tip-top shape. Here are a few hints to help you keep your knives working well:

**Hand-Wash Carbon Steel Knives** as soon as you're finished with them. Then dry them or hang them in a warm place to prevent rusting.

**Remove Corrosion** on carbon steel knives by rubbing them with steel wool or salt and waxed paper. Rinse well and polish with a cotton cloth.

**Never Soak Chef's Knives** or put them in the dishwasher. This exposure to water can split wood handles and dull the blades.

**Store Knives** in a block or magnetic rack so they won't become dull by being tossed into a drawer.

## Experts' Advice

### Sharpening Knives

Sharp, ready-to-use kitchen knives are a must for cooks everywhere. When you're sharpening knives on steel or stone, here's the best approach to use:

- **Hold The Blade** at a shallow angle (about 15 degrees). If knives are held at the wrong angle, the blades may not sharpen.

- **If You're Using** a rotary grinder with small wheels, pull the blades through several times in the same direction so you don't damage the blades.

- **Don't Sharpen** knives with serrated edges.

- **Use The Unglazed Base** of a mug to sharpen knives if you don't have a steel or stone sharpener. Hold the blade at a slight angle and slide it in one direction.

# Keep Flatware Flawless

**Clean Silver Flatware** with silver cleaner. Wash it afterwards. If working in your stainless-steel sink, cover the sink with a newspaper first because silver cleaner will mark stainless steel.

**Remove Egg Stains** from silver flatware by rubbing the piece gently with salt before washing it. Or try a mixture of tomato juice and salt. Rub gently and then thoroughly clean.

**Don't Leave Stainless Steel Flatware** in contact with rhubarb, lemon juice, or vinegar. They all corrode flatware.

**To Prevent Brown Spots** on sterling silver pieces when it's washed in the dishwasher, hand-wash pieces when they're new. This will wash away the surface copper so that it doesn't have time to set when you later expose it to extreme heat in the dishwasher.

**Hand-Polish Silver** with deeply carved patterns by using high-quality silver cream or polish.

**Keep Stainless-Steel** and silver flatware from touching each other in the dishwasher. Place them in separate baskets so that the dishwasher action won't cause pitting.

**Save Time.** Next time you have a crowd over for a special event or holiday, put a colander in the sink where you plan to rinse dishes. After washing the flatware, place it in the colander. Then you can rinse all the flatware at the same time.

# Protect Your Pans

**Wash Aluminum Pans** in mild detergent and water. Rinse with very hot water. Remove dark stains by filling the pan with water, adding 2 tablespoons cream of tartar per quart, and boiling for 20 minutes.

**Remove Pit Marks** from stainless-steel pans with fine steel wool and scouring powder. To keep the items sparkling, polish with a commercial stainless steel cleaner.

**Wash Nonstick Pans** in warm sudsy water. If the black nonstick finish wears off, rub the inside with oil on a paper towel. To remove stains mix 2 tablespoons baking powder, $\frac{1}{2}$ cup chlorine bleach, and 1 cup of water. Fill the pot with the mixture and boil 15 minutes. Wash well, dry, and then rub vegetable oil on the nonstick surface.

**Wipe Cast-Iron** cookware immediately after use and dry it, because it rusts easily. To remove caked-on food or rust, scour with coarse salt and wash in sudsy water. Rinse and dry thoroughly, coat with vegetable oil, and store in a dry place. Put paper towels between stacked pots.

**Wash Pressure Cookers** after each use but don't immerse the cover. This could cause damage. Wipe the cover with a sudsy cloth and rinse it with a damp one. Wash the gasket carefully. Replace it if it's worn because it won't seal in the steam. To clean the opening in the cover, draw a pipe cleaner through the holes several times.

**Wash Copper Pans** in hot, soapy water after using them, or they'll tarnish. Clean copper pans with a paste made from equal amounts of flour, salt, and white vinegar. Keep this paste in a wide-mouth jar with a small sponge for copper-cleaning magic at your fingertips.

**Q.** How do I "season" a new cast iron pan?

**A.** Here's what the experts suggest:

- **Wash the Pan** in sudsy water; let dry.

- **Coat the Inside** thinly with vegetable oil and set the pan in a 325°–350° oven for two hours.

- **Wipe Off the Excess Oil,** rinse the pan, and dry it on a burner set at low heat.

- **Grease It** with more vegetable oil after each use for the first few weeks.

# Beautify Baking Pans and Bakeware

**Clean Discolored Tin** bakeware by boiling it in a solution of white vinegar and water. Soften rust marks with cooking oil. To rust-proof a pan, wipe it all over with buttered paper, and put it in a 350° oven for 15 minutes.

**Remove Sticky Brown Buildup** from baking dishes by spraying them with oven cleaner. After the cleaner has soaked in, wash them in warm, sudsy water.

**Clean Glass And Ceramic** baking dishes with a little baking soda on a damp rag. Scour tough-to-clean dishes with a sprinkle of salt on a damp cotton cloth. Then rinse clean.

**Remove Burned-on Food** from baking sheets by sprinkling baking soda over the area. Add 1 cup of water and soak for several hours. A plastic spatula should lift the final remains. (Note: Don't use this mixture on aluminum pans.)

**Clean Discolored** aluminum pans by mixing 2 tablespoons white vinegar with 1½ tablespoons cream of tartar. Add this to the pan, pour in 4 cups hot water, and heat the pan until it's clean.

**Remove Grease** from enamel broiling pans by covering the bottom of the pan with ¼ cup of water softener. Put a wet dish towel over the pan and let it soak for several hours.

# Bathroom Solutions

Of all the rooms in the house, the bathroom requires more thorough cleaning to keep it sanitized. Keeping it well-ventilated will help because germs and mildew love the warm, steamy environment there. With the right cleaning tools and products, you can keep your bathroom germ-free. In this chapter you'll find advice from the experts at *Better Homes and Gardens*® magazine on:

- **Choosing the best tools** of the trade to keep things spotless
- **Killing germs** and keeping mold and mildew to a minimum
- **Cleaning bathroom surfaces** in a snap
- **Using top tips and tricks** for cleaning the shower stalls as well as shower curtains and doors
- **Cleaning recipes** that work fast on the toilet, sink, and floor
- **Shining mirrors,** fixtures, sinks, and more

## Start in the Bathroom

Along with a "gonna-get-it-done" attitude, open a window for ventilation and turn on your favorite tunes. Time will go by quickly when you're listening to your favorite music, talk radio, or even an audio book. And you'll see fast results and rewards in a small area such as the bathroom.

Another plus: Guests are sure to notice how sparkling clean this area is. A clean, fresh-smelling bathroom area gives the impression of a well-maintained and well-cared-for home. If company's coming, put out potpourri or spray an air freshener in the bathroom before they arrive.

# Tools and Supplies You'll Need

- **Dust Mop.** Sweep up dust and hair before washing the floor. Keep the mop pressed firmly on the floor.

- **Cotton Cleaning Cloths.** Designate special absorbent cotton cleaning cloths strictly for the bathroom.

- **Small Bucket With A Handle.** Tackling the small bathroom floor space is easier if you fill a small bucket with cleaning solution and carry one to each bathroom.

- **Absorbent Paper Towels.**

- **Sponges And A Stiff Brush.** Use sponges on all washable surfaces. Scrub brushes are ideal for cleaning rough surfaces and heavily soiled floors and toilets.

- **Cleansers.** You'll need window cleaner or a vinegar solution for windows and mirrors, disinfectant cleaners for the toilet, and a bathroom cleanser for scrubbing soap scum, lime scale, mold, and mildew.

- **Disinfectant Wipes.** These are handy for wiping off the faucet, countertop, and toilet seat. Clean items in that order.

- **Mops.** A wet mop gets off dirt and grime on large, rough surfaced, washable floors. The mop should be wet but not sopping when you use it. Sponge mops are best for cleaning smooth, moderate-size, washable floors.

- **Plastic Sacks.** Use one to gather trash along the way. Use another to gather dirty cleaning rags that go into the laundry.

- **A Stiff-Bristled Broom** for sweeping floors and a dustpan to collect the dust and dirt. Brooms are terrific for routine cleaning of hardwood floors.

- **Mild Dishwashing Liquid** for general cleaning.

# Beat the Bathroom Blues

Sneaky bathroom germs lurk on countertops, faucet handles, and doorknobs, just waiting for someone to pick them up and spread them. Eliminate germs, bacteria, and a host of other pesky problems with the tips in this chapter.

**Prevent Spreading** flu and cold viruses by washing your hands often and well with soap and water. Tell family members to do the same. (If you can, use a towel to open the door on your way out of the bathroom.)

**Use Waterless Sanitizer** to wash your hands if soap isn't available. It's not as effective as soap and water, but it's convenient and helpful in a pinch.

**Clean Green** with a mixture of 1 gallon hot water and 1 tablespoon bleach. Don't use this around cleaners that contain ammonia; combining the two may cause harmful fumes.

**Don't Use** metal wastebaskets in the bathroom; they quickly become rusty. Wash wicker or plastic waste baskets occasionally. Do it outside with warm, sudsy water and salt; let dry.

# Master Mold, Mildew, Soap Scum, and Mineral Deposits

## Experts' Advice

### Eliminating Mildew

Prevention is the best method for ensuring a mildew-free bathroom. If it's already present, try the following:

- **Remove Mildew** and stains from tub and tiles by wetting the surfaces with water and then spraying them with a solution of 1 cup bleach and 1 quart water.

- **Clean Mildewed** bath mats in the washer with detergent, bleach, and a few colorfast towels to balance the load.

- **Wash Mildewed** shower or window curtains in a mild bleach solution, using 1 tablespoon bleach to every 2 cups warm water.

 **Eliminate Lime Deposits** with a paste of cream of tartar and hydrogen peroxide. Apply it to the deposits, scrub the stain, and let dry. Rinse with clear water and dry again.

 **Remove Stains** from chrome and hard water with a peroxide-base cleaner or a paste of equal parts of hydrogen peroxide, baking soda, and liquid dishwashing detergent. Apply and leave it for 5 minutes. Rinse with clear water.

**Clean Brass** with commercial cleaners, or use a lemon cut in half and then dipped in salt.

**Remove Rust** stains on sinks, toilets, tubs, and tile by using a fresh lemon dipped in salt. The citric acid oxidizes and eats away at the rust. If your tub is white, put bleach-soaked paper towels on the stains and allow them to set for 1 hour.

**Clean Mold** and mildew from grout by using a solution of 1 part bleach mixed with 4 parts water. Sponge or spray it on and let it set a few minutes. Rinse with clear water. Scrub any remaining mildew with an old toothbrush and rinse well.

**If In Doubt** about the kind of cleaner to use on a metallic bathroom surface, call your local home improvement or hardware store for advice.

# Shine Bathroom Surfaces

Follow the manufacturer's instructions when cleaning bathroom surfaces. Acrylic, plastic, and enamel all require different treatments. Know which cleaner they can withstand and never use abrasive cleaners.

**Clean Fiberglass** and acrylic with a mild detergent and a very soft cloth. If the tub is dirty, try powdered laundry detergent. Fill the tub with warm water and sprinkle in laundry detergent.

**Use A Mild** abrasive cleaner for stubborn stains on fiberglass and acrylic. Rub scratches with a little silver polish and then buff back the shine.

**Clean Lime Scale** on fiberglass and acrylic with a mixture of half clear vinegar and half water. Rinse thoroughly and dry with a soft cloth.

**Apply A Thin Coat** of car wax to tile and fiberglass and buff well. This prevents soap buildup.

**Clean Shiny Enamel** with dishwashing liquid and a soft damp cloth. You can use cream cleansers on a really dirty surface, but too much will dull the shine.

**Use Clean Cork** and a little cream bathroom cleanser (equal parts) to scrub stubborn lime scale marks on enamel.

**Remove Stains** from marble-top counters by covering them with a few white paper towels saturated with a hydrogen peroxide solution or full-strength ammonia. Cover the towels with a piece of plastic for at least an hour. Polish the marble after cleaning.

**Clean Stained Porcelain** with a paste of equal parts hydrogen peroxide and cream of tartar. Spread it over the stain, let dry, and rinse off.

**Clean Laminate** countertops or cabinets with a paste of lemon juice and baking soda. You can also use it to revitalize dull-looking laminates. Finish by rubbing them to a shine with a soft cloth.

**Clear Out Medicine Cabinets** regularly and throw away used razor blades and out-of-date items. (Kept too long, medicines may break down and provide inaccurate doses.) Wipe out the cabinet with a disinfectant spray cleaner, rinse, and let dry.

**Use Foaming Tile Cleaner** on bathroom tile. Let it work for a few seconds and whisk away residue with a long-handled brush or sponge. Then rinse and wipe dry.

**Clean Grimy Grout** around the tub area with an old toothbrush dipped in full-strength vinegar or liquid disinfectant.

**Use A Coat** of paste wax on chrome, plastic, fiberglass, marble, and other bathroom surfaces to repel dirt and hard-water deposits.

**Try Rubbing Alcohol** or a chlorine mixture (¼ cup bleach to 1 gallon water) for cleaning caulking around bathtubs.

# Clean Showers Quickly

**Leave Shower Doors Open** after you've showered to allow the air to circulate and dry off surfaces.

**Prevent Streaks** on shower doors by spraying on a clear vinegar and water solution after you've showered. Then buff-dry with a paper towel.

**Squeegee** bathtub or shower tiles to keep them shiny and free of soap scum after the last shower of the day.

**Clean Grimy Bath Mats** with whitewall tire cleaner. Apply the cleaner to the mat outside, and let it soak a few minutes. Then scrub and rinse off.

# Shine Shower Curtains and Doors

Taking a shower is quick and refreshing. Cleaning the shower can be just as easy if you do it regularly. Once dirt and grime have built up, the chore becomes work. With a quick wipe down every day, you won't have to scrub as often.

**Sparkle Up** fiberglass shower doors with a little mineral oil. It removes pesky soap scum.

**Remove Scum** from glass shower doors with a used dryer sheet. There's no lint—and the sheets will help prevent future soap-scum buildup.

**Clean Plastic** shower curtains in the washer on the "delicate" cycle. Use warm water and add bleach to the water. Remove the curtain before the spin cycle begins to avoid rips. Then hang the curtain back in the bathroom to dry.

**Keep Plastic** shower curtains mildew-free longer by soaking them in a tubful of warm water with 1 cup salt added to the mix. Allow curtains to soak for 2 hours and then hang them up to dry.

**If Mildew Lurks** along the bottom of your plastic shower curtain, try cutting it off and see how it looks before you spend money to replace it.

**Extend Shower Curtains** all the way across the shower rod after showering. This allows the air to circulate and prevents mildew spots.

**Prewash Sprays** can often remove soap and scum buildup from shower curtains. Spray them along the bottom and let the spray soak until the buildup loosens. Then rinse shower curtains with hot water and wipe them down with a clean cloth.

# Q.♦ How do I clean a silk shower curtain?

# A.♦ **Look At The Manufacturer's Suggestion** to see if you should dry-clean it. To clean it yourself, place it on a flat surface and sponge it with a lukewarm solution of soap and water. Rinse with clear water and hang it up to dry.

## Tidy the Toilet

Cleaning the toilet is probably not on the top of your list of fun projects. Here are some simple tips to make the task quicker and easier:

 **Pour ¼ Cup** of bleach in the toilet before you leave the house. While you're gone, it will clean, disinfect, and leave a fresh scent.

 **Pour A Half Gallon** of white vinegar in the toilet tank once a month to keep the bowl ring-free.

 **Clean Toilets Overnight** with denture-cleaning tablets.

 **Use Cola** to remove toilet stains. Pour a can into the toilet and let it sit for one hour to remove stains.

 **Pour A Cup** of baking soda into the toilet bowl weekly to prevent clogging and odors.

# Beautify the Basin

Keeping your bathroom basin beautiful is just the beginning. Keeping it free of breeding bacteria is even better. Here are best bets for having a shiny, grime-free sink:

 **Rub Light Basin Stains** with a fresh-cut lemon.

 **Rub Dark Basin Stains,** including rust, with a paste of borax and lemon juice.

 **Rinse Sinks Daily** with warm water and towel-dry them with your shower towel. It will help prevent water-marks and soap-scum buildup.

 **Clean Drains** by pouring 1 cup baking soda followed by 1 cup white vinegar down the drain. Wait an hour and follow the soda-and-vinegar solution with warm water. When you hear the fizz, you'll know it's destroying the buildup. Do this monthly to keep your drain clean and clear.

 **Clean Sink Stoppers** and plugs by popping them in the dishwasher once a week with a load of dirty dishes.

 **Prevent Hard-Water Clogs** by occasionally pouring ½ cup of equal parts of white vinegar and boiling water down drains.

 **Use Liquid Soap** or natural soap to prevent soap-scum buildup on shower doors and tubs. (It's the talc in bar soaps that causes the buildup.)

# Maintain Fabulous Floors

The bathroom floor takes daily abuse. If you've got linoleum, laminate wood, or ceramic tile, you're lucky. It's much easier to keep the bathroom clean and smelling fresh with flat-surface floors.

 **Sweep The Floor** with a broom first, sweeping the dust and dirt into a dustpan. Empty the dustpan.

 **Wash Linoleum** with warm, sudsy water and dry each section promptly. Remove marks on linoleum by rubbing them gently with medium-grade steel wool dipped in turpentine or paint thinner—but don't scrub.

 **Damp-Mop** vinyl and rubber floors with a mild detergent solution. Polish with water-base latex polish and seal with a water-base sealant.

 **Don't Use** solvent-base cleaners. Dirt on vinyl tiles and rubber flooring can become ingrained in the cracks. Don't use wax polish, paraffin, or turpentine on rubber flooring for the same reason.

 **Damp-Mop Wood Floors** a small area at a time using warm water. Then wipe dry.

# Remember the Mirrors

Mirrors in the bathroom can become laden with hairspray, mascara, toothpaste, and a host of other splatters. It's the one surface in the bathroom that shows a guest just how clean the entire room might be. Try these tips for sparkling mirrors:

**Keep Mirrors Free** from fog by cleaning them with shaving cream regularly.

**Wash Mirrors** with rubbing alcohol and a soft cloth for a quick-and-easy cleanup.

**You Also Can Use** cider vinegar on mirrors. Use paper towels to buff mirrors dry.

**Use Coffee Filters** to clean mirrors for a quick, lint-free shine.

**Eliminate Hairspray Buildup** by using window cleaner wiped clear with newspapers instead of paper towels. Or use a little paint thinner on a cotton ball. (The room should be well-ventilated.)

# Try These Other Handy Tips

**Clean Bathroom Fixtures** with rubbing alcohol for a quick shine.

**Steam It Clean** by running a hot shower for about 10 minutes before you're ready to clean. The steam from the hot water will penetrate mold, mildew, and hairspray deposits for quicker cleanup in the bathroom.

**Detach Decals.** If you're ready to remove those 1970s floral design decals, heat them with a hairdryer while you pry them up with a plastic spatula. If glue remains try petroleum jelly or a glue solvent.

**Take Potted Plants** into the bathroom—they like the condensation. During the summer take the plants into the shower with you. They'll enjoy the extra humidity, and you'll love the "tropical" look.

# Freshen Faucets and Showerheads

Faucets and showerheads come in various designs and finishes. No matter what they're made of, they all need cleaning. Here are hints for keeping faucets and showerheads shining bright and looking new:

**Clean Around Faucets** with an old toothbrush dipped in nonabrasive cleaner.

**Prevent Water Spots** by keeping a dry washcloth handy to buff away water spots on fixtures and eliminate scrubbing later.

**Use A Soft Cloth** and warm water on gold-plated faucets because they can scratch easily.

**Spray Glass Cleaner** on chrome faucets and fixtures. Dry and polish them with paper towels. This eliminates grime and water spots.

**Q.** In our bathroom, one faucet is thick with mineral deposits. How can I remove this stuff?

**A.** **Break Down Deposits** by filling a small plastic bag with dissolved water softener and tying it to the spout. Leave it on 2 hours. Then repeat these steps until the deposits are gone.

**Clean The Showerhead** by unscrewing the head and scrubbing it with an old toothbrush or nail brush. Then poke a toothpick through the holes to clear them. Do this gently so the toothpick doesn't break and become lodged in the showerhead.

**Soak Plastic Parts** of the showerhead in warm water and vinegar (1 tablespoon vinegar to 2 cups water), or rub them with a slice of lemon to remove mineral deposits.

**Conserve Water** and make maintenance easy with one of the new self-cleaning showerheads. Ask your local hardware store for information on where to buy these.

# Bedroom VaVoom

**A**t the end of the day, your bedroom should be your sanctuary—a place for rest and refuge. Keeping this room tidy and welcoming doesn't take much time if you do a little bit each day. Pick up dirty laundry, don't let bedside tables get cluttered, and make the bed every morning. In this chapter the experts at *Better Homes and Gardens®* magazine show you how to:

- **Eliminate dust mites** from your bedding
- **Maintain mattresses** so they wear evenly
- **Perk up pillows** for comfort
- **Launder duvets** and comforters safely
- **Clean furniture,** closets, windows coverings, floors, and more

**Get Three Cleaning Supplies**—a window cleaner, grease cutter, and dusting spray. Store them in your bedroom closet for quick access.

**Remove Musty Odors** by applying fragrance to a few cotton balls and placing them strategically out of sight around the bedroom.

**Deodorize Bedrooms** in winter by putting several drops of essential oil or perfume on the heat registers. As the furnace kicks in, the circulating air will send the fragrance throughout the room.

**Eliminate Dust Mites** from bedding by putting your bedcovers and sheets in a garbage bag and tying it up tightly. Then put the bag in the freezer for an hour. No more mites. Vacuum mattresses every other month to eliminate dust mites. Clean louvered doors by stretching an old sock over a ruler to clean between the louvers. Put furniture polish on the sock before you begin. Then you can dust and polish at the same time.

# Maintain Your Mattress

**Invest In A Stain-Blocking Mattress Pad.** The new ones are made of woven fibers that breathe, unlike the old uncomfortable plastic cases. On new mattresses, these pads may help maintain your warranty.

**Freshen Unused Mattresses,** like those in guest rooms and vacation houses, by sprinkling them with baking soda the night before company arrives. Then vacuum it up the next day.

**Get Rid** of musty mattress odors by putting clean cat box litter on top for several days. Then vacuum away the filler and the unpleasant odor.

**Inspect The Ticking** before hand- or machine-washing feather pillows. If the weave is tight with no weak spots, you may be able to machine-wash your pillows without losing feathers.

**When Drying** feather pillows, put a tennis ball in the dryer with them and set the temperature on the lowest possible setting. They'll fluff up as they dry.

**Wash Foam Pillows** in the washing machine and air-dry them (don't put them in the dryer).

## Experts' Advice

### Hand-Washing Pillows

Some pillows made out of special materials may need to be hand-washed. Here are a few tips on how to do this:

- **Immerse Pillows** in a tub of lukewarm water with 1 ounce of baking soda or soap flakes. Squeeze the water gently through each pillow.

- **Rinse Pillows** by gently lifting them up and allowing them to drain. Repeat the process until the water is clear.

- **Put Pillows** through a short spin in a spin dryer if you have one; otherwise, lay them on a flat surface.

- **Turn Pillows** over several times until they're completely dry. This process could take several days.

**Check The Label** for duvet cleaning directions. Some can be cleaned at home in your washer and dryer. Is the duvet too big for your washer and dryer? Find a laundromat where you can drop off laundry. They'll wash, dry, and fold it for you to pick up later.

**Hang Comforters** and quilts outside in a fresh spring breeze to air them out.

**Dry-Clean Wool Blankets.** Blankets with other fibers may be washed, but use the gentle cycle with the least agitation possible and a short spin.

# Freshen Up Fine Furnishings

**Polish Fine Furnishings** once or twice yearly and then dust them lightly the rest of the time.

**Remove Polish Buildup** from waxed furniture by using a clean rag dipped in a mixture of 1 part vinegar and 1 part water.

# Q.
How do I dust my antique bedroom furniture so I can get in all the crevices?

# A.
**Frequently Dust Carved Furniture** with feather or lamb's-wool dusters, or the dust will cling to corners. If dirt gets stuck in the corners, use a soft toothbrush and brush gently. A soft shoe brush works well too.

**TIP 300**

**Avoid Aerosol** furniture polishes and those with added silicones. They give instant shine, but the film doesn't fill scratches or other surface blemishes as wax does.

**TIP 301**

**Clean Pine And Pickled Or Limed Oak** with a chamois cloth dipped in vinegar and water and then wrung out. Dry and polish with furniture cream.

**TIP 302**

**Dust And Rub** these types of wood frequently: washed oak, mahogany, pine, walnut, beech, and elm. Polish occasionally with a light-colored wax polish. A cheap-and-easy method for cleaning oak and mahogany is to wipe them with a cloth dipped in warm beer.

 **Remove Marks** from cedar and hard woods with extra-fine steel wool, rubbing along the grain. Treat with an exterior-grade wood preservative.

 **Wipe Plywood** with a chamois cloth dipped in warm water and wrung out. Rinse with cold water and dry.

 **Rub Teak** with teak oil or cream—never use wax polish.

# Care for Brass, Iron, and More

 **Wash Lacquered Brass** occasionally with warm soapy water. Remove finger marks with a damp chamois cloth and rub with a soft dust cloth.

 **Clean Wrought Iron** with a damp, sudsy cloth and dry immediately with a clean, dry one. Remove rust from large objects like headboards with a bristle or wire brush. Wipe over the surface with paint thinner on cotton swabs. Don't use water on bare iron—it will rust.

**Brush Or Vacuum** wicker and bamboo regularly to prevent dust from clinging to surfaces. Wash with sudsy water, using a soft brush to get in the crevices.

**Clean Chrome** with a soft, damp cloth. Then polish with a dry one. Sticky chrome can be washed with water and a mild soap or detergent.

# Manage Dresser Drawers

**Tidy Dresser Drawers** during your spring cleaning. Take everything out, vacuum the drawers, and wipe them down with a damp rag and a fresh-smelling cleaner.

**Tighten Dresser-Drawer Knobs** during your spring cleaning. Always open dresser drawers by pulling on both drawer handles at the same time. If a drawer knob loosens, remove the stripped screw. Cover the stripped part of the screw with clear fingernail polish and replace the screw.

**Keep The Contents** of your dresser drawers smelling great by tucking in the sachet of a fragrance you enjoy, such as lavender or vanilla.

**Q.** I love my bedroom furniture but hate the new wood smell. How can I get rid of the odor?

**A.** **Empty Dresser Drawers** and place an opened box of baking soda in each closed, empty drawer for a few days. (Charcoal briquettes and kitty litter work well but are messier.) Once the smell is gone, place a new dryer sheet in each drawer for a few days.

**Line Dresser Drawers** with three liner layers at the same time. When the lining gets dirty or marred with scratches, remove the top layer to expose the new layer.

**Wipe The Insides** of dirty dresser drawers with a vinegar-and-water solution (1 part vinegar to 4 parts water). The vinegar smell will go away as the drawer dries out.

**Dry Clothes Thoroughly** before putting them away in dresser drawers. To prevent mold and mildew in dresser drawers, place a charcoal briquette in one corner of each drawer. It'll absorb the moisture that causes mildew.

**Don't Return** heavily soiled clothing to drawers without laundering them first. The human bacteria in fabric is what attracts textile pests.

**Prevent Moths** from laying eggs in woolens by storing items in zippered plastic storage bags and then placing them in dresser drawers.

# Conquer Your Closets

For fresh, clean, and wrinkle-free clothes, start with a clean and organized closet. Invest in sturdy hangers. Then keep the whole closet well-ventilated to avoid dampness and musty odors.

If you keep clothes and shoes spaced far apart, they'll dry out so you won't have to worry about mold, mildew, or moths. Here are more tips:

**Organizing And Cleaning** one closet takes about two hours. This could generate dust, so vacuum the floor and shelves before you sort things and put them away.

**Tie Several** scented dryer sheets to coat hangers in your closet. The scent will freshen up the closet without being overpowering.

**Keep A Box** of dryer sheets in the closet and stuff one in each shoe as you take off your shoes at the end of the day. They'll be refreshed and ready for the next wearing.

**Use Furniture Polish** on patent leather shoes to give them a just-buffed shine.

**Pack Out-of-Season** wardrobe items in storage boxes or suitcases while they're not in use. You'll have more room in your closet that way. At least twice a year, go through all items to see what to keep and what to donate.

**Discourage Moths** in closets with sachets of dried lavender or cedar bark. Don't let the cedar chips touch clothes. They can turn items yellow.

**Don't Store** dry cleaning in plastic bags. Items may turn yellow from the chemicals used in the dry-cleaning process.

**Mop Up Musty Smells** in noncarpeted closets with a solution of 1 gallon warm water, 1/2 cup vinegar, and 1/4 cup baking soda.

# Clean Windows, Blinds, and Floors

It's much easier to clean windows, blinds, and floors on a regular basis than to wait until a thick film builds up. In fact, clean them frequently, and they'll take on a luster that adds warmth and beauty to your home. Try the tricks the experts suggest:

**Wash Windows** on an overcast day for best results. Sun shining directly on the glass causes streaks.

**Avoid Scrubbing** dirty windows with a dry cloth; it will scratch the glass.

**Dust Blinds** occasionally with a vacuum cleaner, or put on cotton gloves and wipe blinds by hand. If blinds are thick with dust, put on old fabric gloves over rubber gloves. Dip your gloved fingers into a cold-water-and-ammonia solution—1 teaspoon ammonia to 1 quart water. Then run your fingers and thumb along each slat.

**Wash Vinyl** or metal blinds with two pails of water—one with household cleaner or ammonia in it, the other with clear rinse water. Fully extend the blinds with the slats set horizontally. Starting at the top wipe each slat with a sudsy sponge. Then rinse with clear water and a fresh sponge.

**Spray Wooden Blinds** with furniture cleaner and wipe with a soft cloth. Don't wash them because the wood may splinter if it's too wet.

**Remove Fly Specks** from painted window frames with cold tea, or use a soft cloth dipped in a mixture of equal parts skim milk and cold water. A rough cloth takes off fly specks better than a smooth one.

# Make Floors Fantastic

**Clean Carpets** by mixing 4 tablespoons regular baby powder, 3 tablespoons cornstarch, and 1 cup baking soda. Sprinkle a thin layer over the carpet in the bedroom and let it sit overnight. Then vacuum it up the next day for a fresher carpet that's even brighter than before.

**Don't Apply Wax** to wood floors with a hard-seal finish. They could become extremely slippery for wet or stocking feet.

**Clean Pet Accidents** with a mixture of 1/2 cup distilled white vinegar and 2 cups water. Wet the area with the vinegar-and-water solution. Then sprinkle the "accident" area with baking soda and scrub it well. When the effervescent action stops, rinse well with warm water and dab dry.

# Sparkling Walls and Ceilings

J ust like other cleaning, the more often you clean ceiling and wall surfaces the better. Light colors require more maintenance than dark ones since dirty finger marks and spots show up more. In this chapter the experts of *Better Homes and Gardens®* magazine bring you information on:

- **General care** and cleaning of walls and ceilings
- **Special easy-to-clean** paints
- **How to clean** washable wallpapers and nonwashable wallcoverings
- **What works** best on porous surfaces
- **Giving a new look** to ceramic tile and grout
- **Stain removal** for ceilings and walls

**Dust High Ceilings** with a clean, long-handled broom or an extended vacuum hose with a brush attachment. Don't use water until you're ready to wash the ceiling and the walls.

**Keep The Hanging Instructions** for your wallpaper. They may include care instructions you might need later.

# General Care

**Remove Cobwebs** when they're new. Once covered with grease and dust, they're more difficult to remove.

**Or Spray Nylon Net** or cheesecloth with a cleaning-and-dusting spray, wrap it around the end of a yardstick, secure it with a rubber band, and use it to remove cobwebs in high corners.

## Experts' Advice

### Safety Tips for Washing Walls

This task is a big one. Here are a few tips:

- **Wear Comfortable Old Clothes** that aren't so baggy, that they catch on the ladder or prevent you from seeing the rungs and buckets underneath.
- **Cover Your Wrists** with sweatbands to catch the drips.
- **If You're Reaching High,** use a stepladder or make sure your support is firm.
- **Wear Rubber-Soled Shoes** for climbing ladders or chairs.
- **Don't Use Water** near electrical wall sockets and lights. You could get an electric shock.
- **Disconnect Electrical Appliances** before you begin.
- **Don't Leave** the bucket at the foot of the ladder where you could step into it. Move the bucket before moving the ladder.

# Spiff Up Those Special Paints

Special paints can make a home look like a designer did the decorating. While they look terrific they also can pose problems for removing spots. You can clean most walls with sponges soaked in all-purpose household cleaner or a homemade solution *(see below)*. To clean ceilings and walls that have special paints follow these directions carefully:

**Use A Homemade Solution.** Mix a homemade solution of 2 tablespoons of ammonia or vinegar and 1 quart of warm water. You can use this all-purpose household cleaner on most walls.

**Another Cleaning Mixture** is 1 cup ammonia, $\frac{1}{2}$ cup vinegar, and $\frac{1}{4}$ cup baking soda in 1 gallon warm water. (Test the cleaning solution on an inconspicuous part of the wall before starting your cleaning project.)

**Remove Surface Dirt** on latex-painted walls by brushing, washing, or vacuuming. Clean small areas in corners and around light switches with a nonabrasive cleaner. Wipe down sills with a lint-free rag moistened with rubbing alcohol.

**Get Rid** of scuff marks on latex paint with a homemade cleaning solution *(see above)*, or apply a paste of baking soda and water and rub lightly with fine steel wool.

 **Wash Oil-Base** painted walls with warm water and soapless detergent, or with one of the homemade cleaning solution on *page 94*. When washing oil-base paints, use a drier cloth than you use for washing latex paints.

 **Add Borax** to the water when cleaning walls painted with textured oil-base paint (1 ounce borax to 1 pint water). Rinse with clean water.

 **Remove Stains** with a commercial paste cleaner, mild scouring powder, or a paste of equal parts baking soda and water.

 **Keep Cleaning Solution** from becoming too dirty by using two pails instead of one. Put cleaning solution in one and leave the other empty. Wring out your cloth or sponge into the empty pail instead of back into your cleaning solution.

 **Use White Bread** to remove finger marks from painted walls. Roll up a slice of bread and dab firmly on the wall marks.

 **Avoid Smoking Inside** if you want your paint job to last longer. Smoking will eventually cause a gray film to form over painted walls.

# Win With Wallpaper

Wallcoverings can make a dramatic impact on a room. They're especially affordable and easy to put up for a quick room makeover, but they're not maintenance-free. Keep your wallpaper looking fresh with these quick tips from the experts of *Better Homes and Gardens*® magazine:

## Caring for Washable Wallcoverings

**Clean Textured** vinyl wallcoverings with all-purpose cleaner. Or you can make a homemade solution of 2 tablespoons ammonia or vinegar and 1 quart warm (never hot) water. Apply the cleaning solution with a thick absorbent cloth. Wait about 15 minutes and then rinse thoroughly with clean water.

**Dust Vinyl Wallpaper** and/or damp-mop it frequently. Dirt tends to make wallpaper brittle if left untreated. Commercial dry-cleaning fluids can be used on vinyl. Using lacquer solvents can melt the surface of the wallcovering.

**Use A Small Brush** on embossed wallcoverings to remove thickly encrusted dirt from the folds.

**Q.** How can I remove a greasy handprint on the new washable wallpaper in my kitchen?

**A.** **Sponge the Soiled Area** with mild liquid soap and cold water. Rinse with clear, cold water. Then wipe it dry with a clean, absorbent cloth. Do a patch test on the wallpaper before washing it in case the color runs.

# Caring for Nonwashable Wallcoverings

**Use a Brush to Clean** ordinary wallpaper because washing it could cause damage. Brush it occasionally with a soft brush or broom head covered with a dust cloth. You also can use a handheld vacuum with a soft brush attachment.

**Rub Marks Gently** with a damp cloth. Then pat the paper dry. Be careful not to rub the paper dry, or the surface will come off in tiny rolls.

**Clean Nonwashable Papers** with a commercial dough-type wallpaper cleaner, gum eraser, or crustless lumps of stale rye bread. Rub the wall with wide sweeping downward movements. Don't rub up or sideways. As the dough, eraser, or bread picks up dirt, turn it so a clean area is always on the outside. Work carefully.

**Make Dough-Type Wallpaper Cleaner** by mixing 2½ tablespoons household ammonia and 1¼ cups water in the top of a double boiler. Add 2 cups flour and 4 teaspoons baking soda. Cook over low heat about 1½ hours. Cool. Store in a tightly sealed jar or a bag that seals.

**Sponge Heavier Nonvinyl Papers** with mild white soap suds on a soft sponge squeezed very dry. Use a light touch to blot the paper and very little liquid. Then pat dry with a clean cloth.

# Fabric-Covered Walls

**Check Instructions** provided by the fabric covering manufacturer. If you don't have the directions, take a swatch of the wallcovering to a dealer for cleaning recommendations.

**Dust Walls** with a clean feather duster or a soft clean rag, then vacuum with a vacuum cleaner dusting attachment or a handheld vacuum.

**Spot-Clean** stains with a soft bristle brush or sponge soaked in a mild detergent-and-water solution. Rinse well. Always test a small area first to make sure the fabric will dry without leaving a watermark.

# Wood Paneling

**Dust Wood Paneling** with a sponge rinsed out in diluted detergent, or polish it with a liquid wax.

**Clean Unwaxed,** varnished, or shellacked wood paneling with a mixture of $\frac{1}{4}$ cup gum turpentine and $\frac{1}{4}$ cup boiled linseed oil (not steam-distilled). Apply and leave on for 15 minutes, then rub off.

## Experts' Advice

### Cleaning Painted Wood Paneling

Painted wood paneling, particularly if the color is light, is susceptible to showing handprints and finger marks. To clean these without pulling off the paint, follow these tips:

- **Dust The Paneling** with a soft clean rag or vacuum it with a vacuum cleaner brush.

- **Use Only A Mild Detergent** solution. Abrasive cleaners may scratch and mar the surface.

- **Eliminate Fine Scratches** on wood paneling by rubbing them in the direction of the grain with clear wax on a damp cloth.

- **Remove Tough Stains** with mineral spirits. Test the area first, using a soft cloth to apply the spirits to an inconspicuous spot. If the mineral spirits don't stain, moisten the cloth with mineral spirits and lightly dab the stain. Allow to dry.

**Use A Small Amount** of shoe polish, dark wax polish, or commercial wood stain to touch up discolored paneling. Buff to a fine finish.

**Cork Coverings** shouldn't get too wet. They'll swell and lift from the wall. If you're worried about cork becoming dirty, treat it with polyurethane sealer to make it like a washable wallcovering. Then you can clean it with a solution of 2 tablespoons distilled white vinegar to a gallon of water.

**Clean Grease** from cork with water containing borax or with a mild detergent solution containing a few drops of household ammonia.

# Beautiful Brick

**Brush And Vacuum** unsealed brick walls twice yearly. Pull out loose grit as you go along.

**Clean Stained Brick** by spraying foam bathroom cleaner or a solution of equal parts of bleach and water directly onto the brick. Clean with a damp cloth. Where necessary, use a scrub brush. Wash gently if the bricks are soft and porous, taking care not to soak them.

 **Remove Crayon Marks** on bricks with a gum eraser.

 **Clean Grease Marks** from brick surfaces by sponging them with small amounts of paint thinner.

 **Use Polyurethane Sealer** to protect bricks. Then you can wash them with a detergent-and-water solution.

 **Clean Soot-Damaged Brick** with alkaline cleaners. Contact a professional restorer to evaluate the brick and determine whether this is the best cleaning method for your project.

# Shiny Mirrors

 **Use Liquid Glass Cleaner** for quick cleanup of day-to-day dirt. Don't spray the cleaner directly on the glass. Instead, spray it on a soft cloth and then wipe the mirror.

 **Wipe Soiled Mirrors** with a solution of 2 tablespoons vinegar, 2 tablespoons rubbing alcohol, and 1 quart water.

**Never Use Ammonia** products to clean mirrors. When the silver backing along the edge reacts with the ammonia, it may result in a black edge forming around the mirror.

**Use A Lint-Free Cloth** and rubbing alcohol to clean mirrored walls. You won't have streaks, and your mirrors will stay cleaner longer.

**Don't Allow** the edges of mirrored tiles to get or stay wet for very long. Moisture will ruin the mirror on the back.

# Classy Ceramic Tile

**Remove Loose Dirt** by sweeping or vacuuming. (Do this immediately after tile is installed and before cleaning.)

**Treat Ceramic Tile** as you would oil-base paints. Wash it with warm water and a few drops of dishwashing detergent.

**Try A Homemade Cleaner** on ceramic tile. Mix 2 tablespoons ammonia or vinegar and 1 quart warm water.

 **Rub Soap-Splattered Tiles** with a cut lemon. Leave for 15 minutes and then polish with a soft cloth.

 **Buff Ceramic Tile** dry after you've cleaned it to prevent streaks.

 **Clean Stained Grout** with a solution of 1 part chlorine bleach and 4 parts water. Apply the solution with a toothbrush and let it sit for 15–20 minutes. Be sure to rinse well.

 **Spiff Up Discolored Grout** by rubbing it with a toothbrush dipped in a commercial bathroom cleaner or in a half-and-half solution of chlorine bleach and water. If the stain won't clean up, it's better and easier to regrout.

 **Manage Mildew** by applying a solution of 1 part bleach and 4 parts water. Scrub hard-to-remove mildew with a toothbrush and rinse.

 **Spray A Hydrogen Peroxide Solution** on heavily soiled grout. Scrub with a grout brush and repeat if necessary. Don't repeat this more than five times, or the solution may begin eroding the grout.

# Straightforward Stain Removal

**Remove Grease Marks** from wallcoverings by making a thick paste from equal parts of baking soda or talcum powder and dry-cleaning fluid. Spread the mixture evenly onto the wall, starting outside the stain. Let it dry and then use a soft brush to wipe it off. Two or three applications may be necessary.

**Remove Nicotine Stains** on walls by dipping a rag into a bucket of distilled white vinegar. Wash the walls from the bottom up so you don't get streaks running down the walls from the solution.

**Rub Permanent Marker Stains** with a dry cloth and toothpaste. For enameled walls hair spray works well. Be sure to hold a cloth underneath the spot before you spray, or the dissolved marker will run down the wall and stain it.

**Clean Up Grease Marks** on new plaster with a sponge dipped in paint thinner.

**Use A Dab** of shoe polish to remove small stains. Choose a shade that matches the ceiling color. White shoe polish on a white ceiling works well.

**Q.**◆My son has had posters on the walls of his bedroom for years. How can I get the tape and glue off the walls without damaging the surface?

**A.**◆ **Put Oil-Free Nail Polish Remover** on the masking tape to soften the glue base. Then lift the top edge and pull it back on itself. Also try running a hair dryer along the tape as you pull it off. The warm air softens the glue.

**Remove Tape Marks** on wallpaper by applying oil-free nail polish remover. Then absorb the residue with a warm iron over a paper towel.

**Clean Silk** wallcoverings only with professional dry-cleaning help.

**Remove Stains** from grasscloth and burlap by rubbing the surface gently with talcum powder. Leave it for a couple of hours and then brush off gently. Don't use dry-cleaning fluids or upholstery cleaners unless you've first done a color test.

# Winning Windows and Floors

t's a great feeling to look out a freshly cleaned window or to watch the sunshine dancing on a fabulously clean floor. The *Better Homes and Gardens®* magazine experts have found easy ways to stay on top of dirty windows and floors with little effort. This chapter will give you insight on:

- **Tools and timing** for cleaning windows
- **What works** for windows—inside and outside
- **How to clean** screens
- **What cleaners work** on various types of floors
- **Carpet-cleaning tactics** and more

## Window-Washing Wisdom

Windows are quite possibly the hardest thing in the house to keep clean. With weather on the outside and living inside, they need regular cleaning. Don't wait for the grime to build up, or the task will take longer. Washing windows frequently gives them a luster and gleam that adds beauty to your home.

**Clean Windows** on an overcast day to avoid smears. The sun shining on the window as you're cleaning causes unsightly streaks.

**Use Windshield-Wiper Fluid** to clean windows, appliances, and no-wax floors. It's less expensive than most conventional cleaning solutions.

**Used Tea Leaves** can be recycled to make a terrific window and pane cleaner. Add them to a little water and wipe down windows and panes with a soft lint-free cloth. Use this solution on wood window panes, not light-colored painted panes.

**Clean Large Areas** of glass with a squeegee instead of cloths. Start at the top and work down the glass, frequently wiping the squeegee blade on a cloth to limit streaking. Spray the window cleaner or water onto the glass at the top of the window and wipe across horizontally. Wipe the squeegee blade on a cloth after each stroke. Repeat for rinsing. Use a toothbrush or cotton swab to get dirt out of all the corners.

**Use Vertical Strokes** to wash your windows on one side, and horizontal strokes on the other side. That way, you'll know on which side of the glass streaks remain.

**Make Your Own** window cleaning solution by mixing 2 tablespoons household ammonia or white vinegar with 1 quart warm water.

**Use A Chamois Cloth,** lint-free linen dishcloth, newspapers, or paper towels to clean windows.

## Experts' Advice

### Caring for a Chamois Cloth

Chamois is natural leather that dries surfaces without leaving spots, streaks, or watermarks. It's pliable, holds as much water as desired, but wrings almost dry for polishing.

- **Don't Use** powdered cleaners or liquid detergents to clean windows if you're using a chamois. Detergents will destroy it.

- **Wash A Chamois** with warm water and soap flakes after using it. Then rinse it out well in clean water.

- **Squeeze The Cloth Gently** and shake it out flat.

- **Allow It To Dry Slowly** away from direct heat and sun.

- **Crumple And Rub** the chamois when it's dry to bring back the softness.

**Use Commercial Window Cleaners** for easy application. They're available in aerosol, spray, or liquid formulas.

**Use Flat Razor-Type** paint scrapers or a safety blade on windows to remove dried-on paint. Always work in one direction. Make a forward stroke, lift the tool off the glass, then make another forward stroke. Never scrape backward and forward; you may scratch the glass.

# Window-Washing Outside

**Keep The Ladder** from slipping when washing windows by placing it on a piece of strong board on soft ground. Nail a piece of wood to the board to steady the ladder. Never use a ladder in a strong wind.

**Remove Screens** and brush them with a vacuum cleaner brush or with a stiff-bristled brush.

**Hire A Professional** to clean windows that are hard to reach or very high off the ground.

**Don't Sit On Window Ledges** and lean out to clean upstairs windows. You could fall.

**Hang The Wash Bucket** on the ladder using an S-hook, available from hardware stores, or use a ladder with a platform. Don't hold the bucket while cleaning or perch it on a narrow window ledge.

**Clean From The Inside Out.** You may be able to clean the outside of the windows from the inside of your home by using a squeegee with an extendable and angled handle.

# Window-Washing Inside

**Wash Window Panes** from the top in horizontal rows. While the panes are still wet, wipe them with a clean cloth soaked in rinse water, squeezed out.

**Rinse Windows** with clear water. If you're using anything other than clear water to wash the windows, be sure to rinse the windows well to avoid a filmy residue.

**Q.**◆Without replacing windows, how can we keep the UV rays from fading furniture?

**A.**◆ **Install Ultraviolet Filters** yourself and follow these tips:

- **Don't Touch Windows** for a month after installing filters. You may damage them.

- **Avoid Adhesive Tape** because it can destroy the coating.

- **Use Chamois Cloths** or paper towels to clean the filters.

 **Small-Paned Windows** don't show the dirt like large expanses of plate glass so they don't need cleaning as often.

 **Clean Stained Glass** as you would window panes. Clean the corners with cotton swabs dipped in cleaning solution.

 **Don't Wash Painted** stained glass because the paint is often loose and can be dislodged easily. Dust with a very soft paintbrush or cloth instead.

# Speedy Window Cleanup

Dirty screens not only block out sunlight but also cause spots on windows when it rains. Follow this expert advice to keep screens clean of dust, grit, and grime with little time spent:

 **Use A Marker** to write a number on the window or door frame and then mark the screen with the same number. It will make it much easier to put each screen back when you're done.

 **Brush Or Vacuum Screens** periodically without removing them. Take them down to wash them.

**Wash Screens** by laying them flat on a smooth surface, such as a picnic table topped with a plastic tablecloth. Scrub them gently with a brush and hot, sudsy water. Then rinse with a hose and shake off the excess water.

**Soak Screens** for an hour before scrubbing so the loose debris falls off. With less scrubbing you'll save time and you won't damage the screens.

**Use Nylon-Covered Sponges** to clean screens. They won't catch on jagged edges and fall apart like a normal sponge.

**Use a Homemade Cleaning Solution.** Mix 2 tablespoons liquid dishwashing soap, 1/4 cup ammonia, and 2 tablespoons borax to make a homemade screen cleaning solution. Soak screens with a yard sprayer hooked up to your garden hose or with a sponge dipped in water. Then dip the sponge in the solution and scrub screens gently. Tap window screens on an old towel to remove the soapy, dirty water. Rinse the screens again and replace them in the windows to air-dry.

**Fill Tiny Holes** in screens with a spot of clear nail polish. This will keep insects from crawling through the holes.

# Handling Hardwood Floors

If you keep your floors dirt-free, the rest of your house is easier to maintain and looks cleaner and more beautiful. Dry-mop often to pick up dust and grit. Pay particular attention to the entryways and hallways where most of the dirt is carried in.

**Remove Ground-In Dirt** on wood floors by gently scraping the dirty area with an old knife, working with the grain. Then rub with paint thinner. Apply polish when you're done, give it time to soak in, and then buff.

**Seal Hardwood Floors** with a sealer and/or water- or wax-base polish to protect them.

**Damp-Mop Wood Floors,** a small area at a time, using warm water. Wipe each area dry before continuing.

**Use A Liquid Cleaning Wax** containing turpentine or nontoxic dry-cleaning fluid for a more thorough cleanup of hardwood floors.

**Try A Homemade Polish.** Mix 1 tablespoon beeswax with 2 cups mineral oil. Melt the mixture in a double boiler. Allow it to cool before using it on wood floors. Apply it with a soft cloth as you would any floor-polishing agent.

# Floor Care

**Shine Wood Floors** by wrapping wax paper around a broom or mop head. Rub the head over the floors for a quick sparkle.

**Put Carpet Runners** over high-traffic areas to protect the wood floors underneath.

**Clean Up Wood Floors** with a quart of strong tea. Brew the tea and let it cool to room temperature. Dip a cloth in the tea, wring it out well, and wash the floor. No rinsing is required. It's the tannic acid in the tea that leaves the shine.

**Repair Scratches** with crayons in corresponding colors to your floors. Test and blend colors to find the right shade. Use a hair dryer to warm the crayon and buff the area with a soft cloth after the crayon has been applied. Buff and reapply if necessary.

**Use Oils** from the corresponding nuts to cover scratches on walnut and pecan floors. Break the nut in half and apply to the scratch. Buff and reapply if necessary.

**Use Iodine** to cover scratches on darker wood floors. Brush it on and buff with a paper towel.

# Vibrant Vinyl and Other Special Floors

Special floors require special care. Check with your installer to see how best to deal with dirt, scuffs, and other marks. If your floors have been down a while, here are a few tips from the experts on keeping floors clean without harming the surface:

**Damp-Mop Vinyl** with a mild detergent solution. Polish it with water-base latex polish and seal it with a water-base sealant.

**Mop Cork Floors** occasionally if they're already sealed. If they're polished, apply a coating of wax polish sparingly no more than twice a year. Sealed cork that's in bad condition can be sanded and resealed. Don't get cork too wet, because it may crack. Always dry the floor thoroughly after washing it.

**Wash Linoleum Floors** with warm, sudsy water and dry each section quickly. Don't wash linoleum more than twice monthly or it may become brittle. Remove marks by rubbing stains gently with medium-grade steel wool dipped in turpentine or paint thinner; don't scrub. Use an oil-base sealant for protection.

**Mix Equal Parts** turpentine and milk to put a shiny finish on old linoleum floors. Allow the mixture to dry and buff with a soft cloth.

**Don't Use** solvent-base cleaners or polishes on vinyl tiles and rubber flooring. Don't use wax polish, paraffin, or turpentine on rubber flooring.

**Use As Little Water** as possible on self-adhesive floor tiles. Water can get in between the seams and unseal the tile.

**Clean Straw Mats** with a homemade solution. Mix ½ cup salt, ½ cup water softener, and ¼ cup lemon juice with 1 gallon warm water. Sponge the mixture on the mat and allow it to air dry.

**Wash Sealed** concrete floors with a damp cloth or mop and a little dishwashing soap. Don't use soap on unsealed concrete or brick floors, because the soap residue is difficult to rinse off.

# Cleaning Marble, Tile, Slate, and Terrazzo Floors

**Damp-Mop Marble Floors** weekly with clear water or a mild detergent and water. Wipe streaks and dirt with a damp sponge and buff-dry. For stubborn dirt use dry borax and a damp cloth. Rinse with warm water and buff dry.

**Remove Stains** on marble floors by rubbing a paste of baking soda and lemon juice on them. Rinse with clear water and dry immediately.

**Treat Newly Laid** quarry-tile floors with linseed oil. Don't wash them for at least two weeks to let the oil soak into the tiles. Damp-mop with warm sudsy water and scrub if necessary.

**Remove White Patches** on newly laid tiles with a weak solution of vinegar and water. Rinse with clear water. (The patches are caused by the lime in the cement or grout.)

**Wash Slate And Stone** floors with a mild detergent in warm water. Apply lemon oil to slate after it has been washed and dried to give it a lustrous finish. Protect stone floors with a cement sealer and wax polish.

**Sweep And Damp-Mop** terrazzo floors as necessary. Use a mild detergent rather than alkaline cleaners such as ammonia or borax, as those can dull the surface. Avoid abrasive cleaners, because they'll scratch the surface.

**Wash Waterproof Varnished Floors** with warm, soapy water. For nonwaterproof varnished floors, damp-mop with a mild detergent solution.

# Carpet and Rug Care

All rugs and carpets get dirty. No matter how careful you are, dust from outside, soot from the street, or food crumbs land on the best-maintained floors. If you've got kids and pets, your carpets and rugs will probably need cleaning more often. Vacuuming regularly raises the nap on carpet and feels great underfoot. Here are some ideas from the experts of *Better Homes and Gardens*® to keep carpets and rugs clean:

**Routinely Maintain** your carpet to extend its life. Vacuuming is the most efficient way of cleaning carpets. It diminishes wear and tear and reduces the need for frequent shampooing.

**Use A Vacuum** with a beater brush—either an upright or a cylinder tank with a power nozzle. The brush agitates carpet fibers and loosens dirt so it can be sucked away easily.

**Vacuum Main Living Areas,** halls, and stairs often. Don't wait until the carpet looks dirty. When vacuuming stairs always start at the bottom and work up. That way you won't grind the dirt into the carpet.

**Oriental Rugs** need special care. Vacuum them regularly and be sure to go back and forth with the nap of the rug. If you use a vacuum with a beater brush to clean Oriental or area rugs, be extra cautious not to damage the fringe.

## Experts' Advice

## Best Vacuuming Tips

Vacuuming is one of the easiest tasks to make your home look tidy and well maintained. Try these tips for best results:

- **Pick Up Debris,** especially buttons and metal objects that could damage the vacuum cleaner hose or belt.

- **Use A Bare Floor Brush** attachment for bare floors, indoor-outdoor carpets, and other carpeting with low pile. For stairs use the small upholstery attachment.

- **Use A Crevice Tool** to clean around chair legs and furniture bases, at the edge of carpeting, and in corners.

- **Vacuum Slowly** and evenly with overlapping parallel strokes.

- **Be Careful** with vacuums that have bumper plates. They can leave scuff marks on furniture legs. You can cover these marks with shoe polish in a color matching the wood.

- **To Unblock** a vacuum hose, unwind a metal coat hanger and use the "hook" to remove the blockage.

**Deep-Clean** carpets yearly. You may want to dry-clean or shampoo the traffic areas more often, particularly if you have children or pets.

**Wash Small Throw Rugs** in a washing machine. Read the labels for care instructions.

**Q.** My daughter knocked a burning candle over on our new living room carpet. How can I clean up the wax?

**A.** **Let the Wax Dry.** Chip off the excess wax with a spoon. Then place a paper towel on the area. Hold a warm iron on the paper towel a few seconds to absorb the wax. Repeat the process until all of the wax is absorbed.

**Vacuum Carpet Tiles.** Treat carpet tiles with carpet cleaner to remove stains. If individual tiles are hopelessly stained, remove and replace them.

**Remove Carpet Indentations** by rubbing the areas with the edge of a small coin. Or lay a wet terry cloth towel, folded twice, over each flattened area. Then steam gently with a warm iron to lift the pile.

**Make Homemade Carpet** and rug shampoo. Mix 1/2 cup powdered or liquid detergent, 1 teaspoon ammonia, 1 teaspoon vinegar, and 1 quart warm water. Mix the solution in a bowl with a hand mixer. Clean carpets and rugs with the froth only. Use a cloth to rub gently over the entire carpet area. Let the carpet or rug dry thoroughly before vacuuming again to raise the nap.

**Remove Carpet Stains** with foamy shaving cream. Apply a dollop to the area. Rub it in well with a cloth or sponge and rinse the area clean. Allow the area to dry overnight and then vacuum it the next day.

**Professionally Clean** stained or soiled Turkish, Oriental, and Persian rugs to avoid potential damage.

**Fade Burn Marks** or scorched areas in any carpet by applying a solution of 1 part hydrogen peroxide and 5 parts water.

**Q.**◆The previous owners of my house had cats that left pet stains on the wood floors. Is there any way to remove the stains without damaging the wood?

**A.**◆ **If The Stains** have been left for some time, they may not come out. Try sanding down the area and refinishing it to match the rest of the floor. If that doesn't work you may have to replace the stained section.

# Fine Furnishings

**W**hether your fine furnishings are antiques you've collected, secondhand pieces from Grandma's attic, or new items, they'll last far longer if you keep them clean and dust-free. In this chapter, the experts at *Better Homes and Gardens*® magazine show you how to:

- **Add a gleam** to wood furniture
- **Care for lacquered** finishes and gilded pieces
- **Season leather** furniture and fix mishaps
- **Clean soft furnishings** and furniture
- **Treat various** soft and hard woods

## Wood-Furniture Care

Let your wood pieces shine. Show them off in the daylight by keeping them spotless and dust free. If you take care of wood, it will last lifetimes for several generations to enjoy. Here is advice from the experts on keeping your wood pieces looking wonderful:

 **Clean And Polish Wood Furniture** with a slightly dampened cloth or a soft electrostatic duster that traps dust. Revive grimy wood furniture with equal parts of olive oil, rubbing alcohol, lemon juice, and gum turpentine. Apply with a soft cloth. Buff with a clean cloth.

 **Use A Soft Toothbrush** to remove dirt in corners. Polish carved furniture with a clean, soft shoe brush. Dust with a feather duster.

**Wipe Up Alcohol Spills** on wood furniture immediately. Rub the area with your hand. The oil in your hand will help restore some of the oil taken out of the wood by the alcohol.

**Q.**◆How can I fix a white heat mark on my wooden table?

**A.**◆ **Choose One:**

- Remove the stain with rubbing alcohol.
- Dab spirits of camphor on the stain and polish with a soft dry cloth.
- Buff the mark with equal parts of cooking oil mixed with cigarette ash.

**Remove Water Rings** by applying mayonnaise liberally over them and letting it set overnight. Wipe the rings off the next day with a soft cloth.

**Banish Water Spots** by using a mixture of 1 cup rubbing alcohol and 1/2 teaspoon lemon oil. Apply the mixture to the affected area. Buff dry immediately to restore the wood's luster.

**Remove Candle Wax** from wood surfaces by heating the wax with a hair dryer set on medium heat. Warm the wax and then quickly wipe it off with a soft cloth or paper towel. Continue until all the wax is absorbed. Clean the surface with a solution of mild distilled white vinegar and water.

**Clean Painted, Varnished, or Sealed Wood** with a sponge dipped in warm water and a mild detergent. Rinse and wipe dry immediately. For bad marks use a cleaning paste. Avoid abrasive cleaners that can damage the surface.

## Experts' Advice

### Try Homemade Polishes

Most furnishings come direct from the factory with a finish in place to protect the surface from daily use. Frequent dusting will keep dirt and grime from becoming permanent. Here are the directions for several homemade furniture polishes:

**Polish #1**–Mix ⅓ cup white vinegar, ⅓ cup turpentine, and ⅓ cup boiled linseed oil and put it in a spray bottle. (Add 4 teaspoons almond extract for a pleasant smell.) Shake well before using. Apply to a damp cloth and buff with another dry, soft cloth.

**Polish #2**–Mix 3 parts olive oil and 1 part lemon oil in a spray bottle. Shake well and use as a furniture polish.

**Polish #3**–Mix 1 teaspoon olive oil with 1 cup white vinegar.

# Laminate, Leather, and Lacquered Furniture

**TIP 465**

**Clean Lacquered Finishes** with a damp cloth only when necessary. Remove finger marks with a damp chamois cloth. Polish the surface occasionally with furniture cream.

## Experts' Advice

### How to Live With Leather

If you've purchased leather furniture, you want to protect your investment and maintain its beauty as long as possible. Here are a few tips:

- **Dust Or Vacuum Leather** upholstery and clean it with saddle soap when necessary. Use as little water as possible. Buff the surface with a soft cloth.

- **Rub Dark Leather** twice a year with castor oil to prevent cracks.

- **Use White Petroleum Jelly** on pale leather.

- **Don't Wax** leather furniture. It doesn't absorb wax.

- **If Leather Furniture Looks Dry,** sparingly apply a commercial leather conditioner. Leave it on 24 hours. Then polish it with a soft, clean cloth. You also can sponge leather with a solution of 1 teaspoon household ammonia, 4 teaspoons vinegar, and 2 cups of water.

**Remove Light Stains** from laminates with a damp cloth dipped in baking soda. Avoid using scouring powders or pads, which can damage surfaces.

**Rid Laminates Of Ink Stains** by applying toothpaste with your finger. Or make a paste of baking soda and water, rub it on, let it set, and rinse the mixture off after a couple of minutes.

**Q.** ◆We have a black ink mark on our reddish leather footstool. Are there any suggestions for getting it off? Help!

**A.** ◆ **Ink Marks Are More Easily Removed** immediately. If time passes, the ink embeds farther into the leather, making it harder to remove. Keep an ink stick on hand for just such accidents. Your best bet now is to use a professional leather cleaner from a reputable furniture store.

**Clean Suede Leather**—the rough undersurface of leather—with a soft brush. Use only made-for-suede leather cleaners. Try an art gum eraser to remove small spots. Keep suede away from sun and heat.

**TIP 469**

**Keep Leather Furniture** out of direct sunlight and away from heat registers and radiators. This will help keep it from getting too dry and cracking.

## Experts' Advice

### Care for Veneers

Treat veneered pieces according to the type of wood in the veneer. Wipe up water spills right away to prevent marks. Check veneered surfaces for bubbling when you clean them. You can repair small blisters in veneer as described below. Call on a professional to repair large blisters.

- **Cut The Blister** along the wood grain with a sharp knife.
- **Using The Knife Blade,** ease some polyvinyl resin adhesive into the cut.
- **Cover The Blister** with aluminum foil, several layers of blotting paper or brown paper, or a folded sheet. Press with a hot, dry iron.

**TIP 470**

**Handle Marquetry** with care. These are veneer surfaces inlaid with wood, shell, or ivory. Dust them gently and try not to catch the inlaid edges with your dust cloth.

**TIP 471**

**Remove Marks** made from candle wax and oils on veneered and inlaid wood by covering the marks thickly with talcum powder. Next cover the powder with several layers of paper towels. Iron with a warm, dry iron.

# Gilded Furniture

**Dust Gilded Furniture** with a feather duster.

**Clean Gilded Furniture With A Soft Cloth** lightly dipped in warm turpentine or paint thinner. (Warm these solvents by standing the bottle in warm water.)

**If The Gilt Is Flaking,** don't try to clean or repair it yourself. Get professional advice.

**Never Rub The Gilding.** If necessary, brush the dust off with a soft watercolor paintbrush. Never let water get onto a gilded surface. To remove stains, dab the surface of an onion gently on the affected area.

# Untreated-Wood Care

Untreated wood is both beautiful and durable when it's new. Preserve its splendor by protecting its natural surface. Keep these things in mind when you're caring for untreated wood:

**Scrub Unpolished** or unsealed wooden tables, butcher block, and chopping boards after each use with sudsy water and a scrub brush. Then rinse and dry them thoroughly.

**Treat Wood Occasionally** with a thin coat of mineral oil on a clean cloth. Don't use vegetable oil, which can turn rancid.

**Clean Bamboo Pieces** with a damp, soft cloth.

**Wipe Cane** with a soft, dry cloth. Have a professional furniture restorer repair tears.

**Brush Or Vacuum Wicker** regularly. Wash wicker pieces with sudsy water and borax, using a soft brush to get into the crevices. If a piece is really dirty, add a capful of ammonia and rinse well after cleaning. Dry outside on a sunny day.

**Clean Glass** with a commercial glass cleaner. Or mix 2 tablespoons vinegar in one quart water. Moisten cloths and wipe glass surfaces. Rinse with clear water and wipe with a dry cloth.

**Use An Ostrich-Feather Duster** for removing dust from delicate surfaces. Avoid inexpensive synthetic dusters. They may scratch surfaces.

**Wipe Rush, Sea Grass,** or twisted fibers with a damp cloth only when necessary.

# An "A" for Antiques

With the proper care and cleaning, antiques can last for several lifetimes and be cherished as they're handed down from generation to generation. Here are some time-tested care tips:

 **Remove Sticky Residue** on antiques with a cloth dampened with white vinegar. Gently rub the area. Then polish with a soft cloth.

 **Banish Musty Odors** by rubbing the inside of any doors or drawers with oil of wintergreen.

 **Use A Lamb's-Wool Duster** on antiques (feather dusters can break off and scratch surfaces).

 **Polish Antiques** only once or twice a year. Apply polish sparingly and evenly. Then rub it in well until a good shine appears. If the polish is too thick, it may leave the surface smeary and difficult to buff.

 **Avoid Polishing** near pieces of wood that are cracking or lifting. If wax gets under them, gluing the loose pieces back will be difficult.

**Don't Use Aerosol Furniture Polish** on antiques. Although it gives an instant shine, it doesn't fill scratches as wax does. With some aerosol sprays, the solvent comes out forcefully enough to damage polished surfaces. If overused, aerosol polish can produce a milky look. There's no remedy for this except stripping and resurfacing.

# Treating Specific Marks

**Remove Black Heat Marks** by rubbing them with a cut lemon to bleach the marks. When the wood is dry, recolor it with a commercial wood stain, scratch cover, or shoe polish. Repolish the surface with a soft cloth.

**Remove White Heat Marks** with rubbing alcohol or paint thinner. When dry recolor the wood with a commercial wood stain, scratch cover, or shoe polish. Repolish the surface.

**Remove Heat Marks** on plastic or lacquered finishes with brass polish. Wipe off the polish before it dries. Then rub the area with a very hot cloth heated in the microwave.

**Remove Black Water Marks** by rubbing the surface gently with fine steel wool until unfinished wood is reached. Recolor or stain the wood. Polish or oil the wood as necessary.

**Remove White Water Marks** by rubbing them with very fine steel wool and oil. Rub with the grain. Apply a half-and-half solution of linseed oil and gum turpentine. Leave the solution on 2 hours. Then remove it with vinegar and buff with a soft cloth.

# Cleaning Soft Furnishings

**Vacuum The Sofa, Chairs, and Cushions** regularly. Clean the armrests, backs, and crevices with the upholstery attachment of the vacuum cleaner. Regular dusting and cleaning will help prolong the life of a sofa or chair.

## Experts' Advice

### Vacuuming Textiles

Textured covers add drama to couches, while fabric pillows and wall hangings create warmth. Here are some tips on care:

- **Use The General-Purpose** vacuum cleaner head to clean textiles. Brushes of any kind can roughen loose threads.

- **Avoid Strong Suction** that can pull out loose threads. Don't vacuum fringes or embroidered items with beads or sequins that could come off.

- **Use A Small Handheld** vacuum cleaner for most textiles. They're far less cumbersome than other kinds of vacuums.

**Deep-Clean Chairs And Seats** occasionally, before they look dirty. Remember that cleaned upholstery will rapidly get grimy again if you don't properly remove all of the detergent or cleaner.

**Use Silicone Sprays** on upholstered furniture to protect the surface. Retreat as recommended.

# Q.◆I've used different fabrics to make my slipcovers and pillows. How do I clean them?

## A.◆ Follow These Care Tips:

- Dry-clean brocade, glazed chintz, silk, tweed, and velveteen.
- Scrub canvas and sailcloth with warm sudsy water; rinse in clear water.
- Launder cotton and linen.

# Objects of Your Affection

**D**ecorative objects sometimes require special attention. They need careful dusting and some require an occasional washing. If the items are valuable, you might want to call a professional for help. Otherwise, try these tips from the experts at *Better Homes and Gardens®* magazine to help you keep your treasures looking good. You'll discover advice on:

- **Cleaning metalwork,** including silver, gold, and platinum
- **Caring for chrome,** brass, copper, bronze, and more
- **Preventing chips** and breaks in china and glass
- **Cleaning** cracks in porcelain
- **Handling stemware** and fragile pieces
- **Removing stains** from vases and wax from candlesticks

## Maintaining Metalwork

Metal surfaces can scratch and wear away easily. Too much polishing can eventually disfigure a metal object. So save yourself some work by cleaning metal items only when they absolutely need it. Or if you have a valuable small piece, take it to a jeweler instead. Otherwise, follow the guidelines below:

**TIP 498**

**Wear Cotton Gloves** when cleaning metal. Otherwise, the acid in your skin will tarnish the metal.

**Use a Professional** cleaner for badly tarnished or dirty antique metal pieces.

**Never Use Silver Cleaner** on metals other than silver, gold, or platinum, unless specified.

**Use a Drop** of paint thinner on a cotton ball to brighten silver pieces that don't hold food.

# Stunning Silver

**Wash Silver Regularly** so you won't have to polish it as often—easier for you and better for the silver. After using silver wash it in hot water and dishwashing liquid as soon as possible. Rinse and dry thoroughly.

**Dust Decorative Silver** pieces regularly and wash them occasionally to keep them bright.

**Remove Small Scratches** on silver pieces by rubbing them with jeweler's rouge, which you can purchase in most jewelry stores.

**Wash And Dry Silver** before polishing it. Rub in the polish with a soft, dry cloth and a small, soft brush to get inside the crevices; rub lengthwise, not crosswise or in circles. Make sure no excess polish is left on the silver—it will cause the silver to tarnish again more quickly. Wash the silver, rinse it, and buff it with a chamois or soft cloth.

**Polish Tarnished Silver** by rubbing it with commercial polish or a paste of equal parts of baking soda and water. Never use abrasive cleaners—they'll scratch the surface. Always polish silver near an open window, because the tarnish may give off a sulfurous gas.

**Q.** How can I polish the small spaces between the tines of the silver forks?

**A.** **Coat a String** with silver polish and rub it between tarnished fork tines. Store your silverware in special bags or rolls of cloth saturated with tarnish inhibitor purchased from a jewelry store.

**Deep-Clean Valleys** or indentations in silver pieces with a cotton swab dipped in a liquid polish. Work the swab into the crevices to remove the tarnish. Rinse well.

# Cleaning Gold, Platinum, Brass, and Bronze

**Dust Gold Pieces** lightly with a clean, dry chamois cloth. Don't use ordinary cloths, because they may harbor grit, which could damage the metal. Take precious gold pieces to a jeweler.

**Clean Low-Karat Gold** with silver polish. When not in use wrap these items in a chamois cloth or acid-free tissue.

**Clean Platinum** with a detergent or a soap-and-water solution, and dab dry. It doesn't tarnish.

**Wash Lacquered Brass** items occasionally in soapy water. Don't polish them—polish can damage the lacquer. If a brass object is very dirty, wash it in a solution of 1 part household ammonia and 4 parts water.

**Clean Dirty Brass** with a lemon dipped in salt or a paste of equal quantities of vinegar, flour, and salt. Rinse off thoroughly; clean with brass polish.

**Clean Brass Ornaments** by boiling them in water containing salt and vinegar. Rinse and dry.

**Clean Brass** door knockers with a soft cloth dipped in ammonia.

**Prevent Tarnishing** on brass by applying lemon oil or car wax.

**Dust Bronze Items** lightly once or twice a year with a soft, clean cloth. Don't use a wire brush or harsh abrasives; they'll damage the surface.

**Have a Professional** clean antique bronze items. Never wash antique or valuable bronze—it can result in rapid corrosion, and cause the metal to start flaking away. Rubbing alcohol should not be used on antique or valuable bronze.

**Remove Verdigris** (greenish-blue deposits) on bronze items by scraping the surface lightly with a knife or rubbing it with a toothbrush. Rinse and dry with a soft cloth.

# Shining Up Stainless Steel, Chrome, and Brass

**Wash Stainless-Steel Pieces** occasionally in hot sudsy water, adding ammonia to the water (2 tablespoons per quart). Soak very dirty pieces in warm sudsy water. Wash sinks, countertops, or stove tops with borax. Avoid abrasives because they scratch the surface.

**Wipe Chrome** with a soft, damp cloth, and polish it with a dry one. Sticky chrome can be washed with a mild dishwashing soap and water solution.

**You Also Can Clean** chrome by polishing the surface with a cloth dipped in apple cider vinegar. Don't clean chrome with harsh polishes; they'll scratch it and damage the shine.

**TIP 522**

**Clean Grease** and grime off chrome with a little paraffin on a damp cloth or baking soda on a dry one. Rub burnt-on grease with baking soda.

**TIP 523**

**Use Furniture Polish.** A thin film of silicone furniture polish helps protect chrome furniture.

**TIP 524**

**Clean The Inside** of chrome teapots with a cloth moistened with vinegar and dipped in salt.

**TIP 525**

**Keep Pewter Dry** or it will develop a gray film and tarnish. Don't disturb the tarnish found on an antique piece; the piece may disintegrate. Call a professional antique dealer for advice.

**TIP 526**

**Polish Pewter** with a suitable metal polish or with a little household ammonia or rubbing alcohol for a bright finish. For a dull finish rub with olive oil or a raw cabbage leaf. Rub badly stained pewter with fine steel wool and olive oil.

**TIP 527**

**Clean Pewter** by applying a paste of equal parts of olive oil and cigarette ash. Rub the mixture on the items and then buff well.

# Glistening Glass and China

**Decorative China,** ceramics, and glassware need careful dusting every couple of months. If they get grimy wipe with a damp, sudsy cloth, then with a clean, dry one.

**Wipe Fine China** on display with a damp cloth, then dry with a linen towel. Never use detergents or bleaches to try to remove stains.

**Clean The Dirt** in cracks on porcelain by dipping a cotton ball in warm water. Squeeze out the excess water and dip it in baking soda. Put the cotton over the crack and let it sit for several days, rewetting the cotton now and then. Then scrub gently with a fine-bristle brush dipped in 1 cup water and 1 teaspoon ammonia. Rinse, dry, and enjoy the piece once again.

**Use a Soft Brush** to clean the grooves on a raised pattern in your porcelain.

**Don't Use** cleaning powders or scouring powders on china or ceramics; they may damage both the glaze and the pattern.

**Glassware With Metal Decorations** should only be dusted. If the glass is very dirty, clean it with a slightly damp cotton cloth and dry it right away. Don't let the metal get too wet.

**Don't Touch Glassware** with painted or gilded decoration. The decoration may not be firmly fixed and could come off. Brush it gently with a soft watercolor paintbrush or a photographer's small lens brush.

# Vibrant Vases and Various Other Objects

**Clean Stains** caused by flower water in vases by filling the vase with hot tap water and adding 4 capfuls of ammonia. Let the vase sit and rinse it with clear water. Repeat if necessary, adding a shot of dish soap. Give it a good scouring and you're ready for the next round of roses.

**Use a Thin Coat** of petroleum jelly to clean cloudy glass. Apply it with a soft cloth and let it sit for 3–4 days. Wash it off with a rag dampened with a solution of water and dishwashing liquid. Polish with a soft, dry cloth.

**Remove Stains,** cloudiness, or mineral deposits in glass vases and decanters by filling them with water containing two teaspoons of household ammonia. Let them soak for a few hours, and then wash well and rinse with clear water.

**Remove Odors** from leather-bound books by placing them in a paper bag with baking soda. Shake the bag several times and then let it sit for a week or more. After 7–10 days, shake the books out well. They should smell much better.

**Q.** What's the best way to clean water spots from an antique glass container?

**A.** **When Hand-Washing It,** pour in a handful of uncooked rice or dried beans. Add a dash of liquid dishwasher detergent, fill with water, and shake. To rinse, fill the vase with cold water. Then turn it upside-down and allow it to empty while cold water from the faucet runs over the base. This gets rid of all the water–and the spots.

**Clean Seashells** and coral pieces in hot, soapy water with a little water softener added. Rinse in cool water.

**Use Baking Soda** on a damp cloth to clean switchplate covers.

**Machine Wash** stuffed animals by putting them in a pillowcase and tying the end in a knot. Run them through the washer and dryer to clean dirt, grime, and odors.

**You Also Can** clean stuffed toys by rubbing a little cornmeal in and letting them sit for over an hour. Dust off or gently vacuum before returning them to their rightful owners.

**Use a Blow Dryer** on the cool setting to get rid of dry dust particles on lead crystal (it scratches easily). To eliminate fingerprints, wipe gently with a soft, lint-free cloth dampened with glass cleaner. Don't crowd or stack the pieces.

# Candlesticks and Knickknacks

**Remove Old Wax** from candleholders by lining a baking sheet with newspaper, then a layer of paper towels before placing the candlesticks upside down on the papers. Preheat oven to lowest setting. Turn off the oven and place the baking sheet inside on the lowest rack. Close the oven door and let sit for 15 minutes to melt the wax. Wipe candlesticks with a soft cloth and discard the papers. Do not use this method on fragile, thin, or antique candlesticks.

**Soften Wax** from various surfaces by covering your finger with a soft cloth. Then peel off the wax gently with your fingernail.

**Remove Wax From Candelabras** by using a blow dryer to melt the wax in the holders. Then pour the wax out into a garbage bag.

**Remove Wax From Carpets** by placing a brown paper sack over the area. Press a warm (not hot) iron on the spot. Keep moving the brown bag so you use a clean part of the bag until you've absorbed all the wax.

**Rub Candleholders** and candelabras with petroleum jelly before using them. That way melted wax won't stick so easily and cleanup will be a breeze.

# Out With Stains

Taking care of fabrics is essential to keeping them in good condition for a long time. Some fabrics require special handling, so always check the care label when buying them or before laundering them. In this chapter the experts at *Better Homes and Gardens®* magazine have taken the guesswork out of caring for fabrics and treating stains. You'll find important information in this chapter on:

- **What care labels** can tell you
- **What laundry products** work best on what kind of stains
- **How to take care** of your laundry-room appliances
- **Caring for special fabrics**
- **How to get out** tough stains

## Laundry Products

**Use Most All-Fabric** bleaches for colored fabrics and most fibers, with the exception of silk and wool. You can purchase bleaches in powder or liquid form.

**Dilute Liquid Chlorine Bleaches** with water before using them. These are the strongest and quickest bleaches. Properly diluted, they are safe for cotton, linen, rayon, and synthetics such as nylon and polyester. Colored clothing, particularly synthetics, may not be colorfast in liquid chlorine bleaches. Check the label for instructions.

# Q.◆Why use pretreatment wash sprays?

# A.◆ **They're More Effective** than regular detergent on very dirty areas, such as shirt collars or underarm areas. Follow the directions carefully. They require from several hours to overnight to work.

## Experts' Advice

### How to Read Care Labels

- **Hot Water:** Water up to 150°

- **Warm Water:** Water between 90° and 110°

- **Cold Water:** Water up to 85°

- **Durable or Permanent-Press Cycle:** Cool rinse before spinning (reduces wrinkling)

- **With Like Colors:** Wash with clothing of similar color and brightness

- **Dry Flat:** Lay out horizontally to dry

- **Block to Dry:** Reshape to original dimensions

- **No Chlorine Bleach:** Chlorine bleach may be harmful

**Enzyme Presoaking Bleaches** work best on organic or protein stains, such as mud, egg, milk, or baby formula. They're not safe for silk, wool, cashmere, mohair, and angora. Wear gloves to avoid skin irritation.

**Use Pretreatment Sticks** and gels on protein stains like grass and baby formula. Apply them directly to the stain as soon as the spill occurs and launder within 3–4 days. Gels work the same way but can be applied up to one week before laundering. However, don't use them on light or fluorescent colors.

# Washer and Dryer Care

Do research before you invest in laundry equipment. Features differ between brands and machines. Once you've found the ideal set, take good care of them and they'll last for years. The experts agree that, with a little care, you can keep your washer and dryer running smoothly and working well. Here are some dos and don'ts for maintaining laundry equipment:

**Add Liquid Fabric Softeners** to the final rinse water in a machine. They make ironing easier by reducing the friction between the fabric and iron. They prevent static electricity from forming on man-made fibers.

**Be Sure** your washer and dryer are properly installed and your dyer is vented correctly so that the machines operate efficiently. Call a professional to check them if you're in doubt.

**Don't Overload** a washer or dryer because the machines won't work as efficiently.

**Wipe the Surfaces** of your washer and dryer occasionally with a damp cloth.

**Keep Machine Doors** open to let the air circulate, except when children or pets are around.

**Don't Use** abrasive cleaners on the outside of your washer or dryer. These may scratch surfaces.

**Use The Right Amount** of laundry detergent, following machine instructions. Measure carefully. Using more than specified will make rinsing more difficult.

**Keep Your Washing Machine Clean.** Wipe out the soap, bleach, or fabric softener compartments regularly. For front-loading machines, wipe the rubber door gasket where water often collects in the fold.

**Q.**◆How often should I remove lint from my dryer?

**A.**◆**After Each Use.** Dryer lint builds up quickly and may start a fire if it's not removed often.

**Check Washer Hoses** periodically by turning the water on and feeling for bulges. Replace hoses that have bulges.

**Check Dryer Doors** for tightness by moving a piece of tissue paper around the door's edge while the dryer is on. Have the seal checked regularly.

**Clean The Dryer Lint Screen** at least every six months with a nylon brush, as follows:

• Wet both sides of the lint screen with hot water.

• Wet a nylon brush with hot water and liquid detergent; scrub the lint screen with the brush to remove residue buildup.

• Rinse the screen, dry it, and replace it.

# A-Z Stain Removal

- **Alcoholic Beverages.** Don't use soap. Wash the item with detergent in water as hot as is safe for the fabric.

- **Baby Spit-Ups.** Apply a liberal amount of water to wet stains. Then sprinkle powdered dishwasher detergent on them and let the item sit for at least 12 hours. Launder as usual.
- **Ballpoint Pen.** Spray or dab the stains with dry cleaning solvent. Then rub them with heavy-duty liquid detergent. Wash the item with detergent and all-fabric bleach. **Note:** On suede, rub ballpoint pen marks gently with fine sandpaper.
- **Beer.** Don't use soap. Wash the item with laundry detergent in water as hot as is safe for the fabric.
- **Bird Droppings.** For fresh stains, use a pretreatment before laundering as you normally would. If the stain has aged, or remains after laundering, soak the stained area for about an hour in an enzyme-based laundry booster.
- **Blood.** Don't use warm water. Dried blood should be brushed off and the item soaked in cold water with heavy-duty detergent for several hours. Then launder as usual.
- **Blueberry.** Pretreat stain with heavy-duty liquid laundry detergent. Rinse. Soak fabric in a diluted solution of all-fabric powdered bleach and water. Repeat until the stain lightens or disappears. Do not dry in the clothes dryer. The heat will set in any remaining stain.
- **Butter.** Pretreat stains with heavy-duty liquid detergent. Wash the fabric in water as hot as is safe for the fabric.

- **Candle Wax.** Freeze wax with ice cubes and break off the frozen pieces. Rub residual stains with dry-cleaning solvent and then with heavy-duty liquid detergent. Wash the item with detergent and an all-fabric bleach.

- **Catsup.** Rub the stain with heavy-duty liquid detergent before washing. Wash the item using detergent and all-fabric beach. If the fabric is colorfast, you can wash it in chlorine bleach.
- **Chocolate.** Scrape off any solid matter. Then rinse the stains with cold water and rub them with heavy-duty liquid detergent. Wash the item with detergent and all-fabric bleach.
- **Clay.** Remove any remaining clay with a soft scraping tool such as a spoon. Soak the stain in clear water for about 20 minutes before pretreating the stain and laundering as usual.
- **Coffee.** Don't use bath soap or dishwashing liquid. Wash the item with laundry detergent.
- **Collar Rings.** Soak stains for 1 hour in a solution of ¼ cup salt, 1 cup vinegar, and 3 quarts warm water. Launder as usual.
- **Cooking Fats and Oils.** Wash the item in heavy-duty detergent and hot water. For difficult stains use a pretreatment product on the stain before washing.
- **Cough Syrup.** Soak garment for 15-30 minutes in 1 quart warm water, ½ teaspoon liquid dishwashing detergent, and 1 tablespoon white vinegar. Rinse thoroughly. Launder as usual.
- **Crayon.** Spray or dab the area with WD-40. Then rub it with heavy-duty liquid detergent. Wash the item with detergent and all-fabric bleach.
- **Cream.** Rinse the item in cold water and wash with detergent.
- **Crude Oil Or Tar.** Treat stains with a petroleum-base solvent pretreatment spray. Then wash the item with heavy-duty detergent and hot water.
- **Curry.** Use an oxygen bleach product in the wash cycle. Allow to air-dry to make sure the stain has been removed. If not, repeat the process.

- **Deodorants.** Apply heavy-duty liquid detergent directly on stains; wash the item in detergent and warm water. **Note:** A buildup of aluminum may be permanent.

- **Diaper Rash Cream.** Scrape away remaining cream with a soft scraping tool such as a spoon. Use a pretreatment prior to laundering as usual. Do not dry. Check the garment again, and repeat laundering process if any stain remains.
- **Dyes.** Marks caused by dyes are difficult to remove. Rinse the area with cold water and treat it with liquid detergent. If the stain persists soak the item in a diluted solution of powdered all-fabric bleach. Then wash it in detergent and bleach.

- **Egg.** Soak the stains in cold water and launder as usual.
- **Engine Oil.** Treat affected areas with a petroleum-base solvent pretreatment spray. Then wash the item in heavy-duty detergent and water as hot as is safe for the fabric.

- **Feces.** Scrape any solid matter off. Soak the item in cold water and launder as usual.
- **Felt-Tip Pen.** Pretreat the area with heavy-duty liquid detergent and rinse well. If stains persist soak the item in a diluted solution of all-fabric bleach. Then wash it in detergent and bleach safe for the fabric.
- **Fruit And Fruit Juices.** Wash with detergent. Or try mixing $\frac{1}{2}$ cup cool water, $\frac{1}{4}$ cup baking soda, and 1 tablespoon borax. Apply the solution to stains and let the item sit for 20 minutes. Rinse in cool water and launder as usual.
- **Furniture Polish.** Treat with a dry-cleaning solvent, then rub with heavy-duty liquid detergent. Launder as usual.

- **Grass.** Mix 2 tablespoons rubbing alcohol, 1 tablespoon glycerin, and $\frac{1}{4}$ cup warm water. Soak the garment for 30-60 minutes and then launder as usual.
- **Gravy.** Rub the stain with heavy-duty liquid detergent. Wash the item with detergent and all-fabric bleach. If the fabric is colorfast, wash it with chlorine bleach.
- **Grease.** Treat stains with a petroleum-base solvent pretreatment spray. Then wash the item with heavy-duty detergent in hot water.

- **Hair Dye.** Loosen the stain with hairspray if it's fresh. Launder as usual.

- **Hair Spray.** Rub stains with heavy-duty liquid detergent. Then wash the item, using detergent and all-fabric bleach. If the fabric is colorfast, you can wash it with chlorine bleach.
- **Hobby Glue.** Scrape away remaining glue with a soft scraping tool such as a spoon. Soak the garment (30 minutes for fresh stains, several hours for set-in stains) in cold water and rinse. Check the garment. If the stain remains, soak another 30 minutes. Rewash. Repeat until the stain has disappeared. Follow garment label warnings and manufacturer's instructions.

- **Ice Cream.** Soak stains in cold water. Launder as usual.
- **Ink (permanent).** Pretreat stains with heavy-duty liquid detergent and rinse well. If stains persist, soak the item in a diluted solution of powdered all-fabric bleach. Wash it in detergent and bleach that are safe for the fabric.
- **Ink (washable).** Wash the stain with detergent. Don't use bleach.
- **Iodine.** Treat stains with sodium thiosulfate (available in photo supply stores as "acid fixer"). If the solution contains other chemicals, don't use it.

- **Jam.** Soak the item in cold water. Launder as usual.

- **Ketchup.** Rub the stains with waterless hand cleaner and rinse the item in cold water.

- **Lipstick.** Treat the stain with dry-cleaning solvent, then wash the item in heavy-duty liquid detergent. Wash it again, using detergent and all-fabric bleach. If the fabric is colorfast, you can use chlorine bleach instead of all-fabric bleach.
- **Liquid Paper.** Blot excess fluid and allow to dry completely. Brush away particles. Use a pretreatment stain remover. Rinse. Rub liquid detergent into the stain, soak, and launder as usual.

- **Makeup.** Rub stains with heavy-duty liquid detergent. Then wash the item, using detergent and all-fabric bleach. If the fabric is colorfast, you can use chlorine bleach instead of all-fabric bleach.
- **Mayonnaise.** Scrape off the excess with a dull knife. Wash the item in heavy-duty detergent using water as hot as is safe for the fabric.
- **Meat Juice.** Soak in cold water. Launder as usual.
- **Mildew.** Brush the item outdoors so mildew won't spread in the house. Pretreat the affected area with heavy-duty liquid detergent and bleach. Wash the item in hot water with heavy-duty detergent safe for the fabric.
- **Milk.** Soak the item in cold water. Launder as usual.
- **Mud.** Soak the item in cold water after using detergent or enzyme presoak. Wash it with detergent as usual.
- **Mustard.** Wash the item with detergent and bleach as safe for the fabric.

- **Nail Polish.** Don't use nail polish remover because it may dissolve some fabrics. Dry-clean the item professionally to be safe.
- **Nicotine.** Blot the stain with eucalyptus oil and launder as usual.

- **Oil-Base Paint.** Pretreat with a heavy-duty liquid laundry detergent or an aerosol petroleum-based solvent pretreatment spray. Launder as usual.
- **Orange Juice.** Fresh orange juice spills can usually be removed by washing in detergent and hot water. Old stains may need to be bleached for removal.

- **Paint (Latex).** For best results treat the area while the stain is still wet. Soak the item in cold water. Then wash it in cool water with heavy-duty detergent. Dried paint is very difficult to remove. Treat it the same as you would treat a stain of permanent ink.

- **Perfume.** Don't use bath soap or dishwashing liquid. Wash the item in detergent.
- **Perspiration.** Apply liquid detergent directly to the stain. Or presoak the garment for 15-30 minutes in liquid detergent and water.
- **Petroleum Lip Balm.** Pretreat with a concentrated grease removal product. Launder as usual.

- **Red Wine.** Dip washable fabrics in a solution of 2 cups warm water and 1 tablespoon borax. Launder the item as usual after stain removal.
- **Ring Around the Collar.** Clean soiled shirt collars by pretreating with shampoo. Launder as usual.
- **Rust.** Don't use chlorine bleach; it sets the stain. Treat the affected area with a commercial rust remover.

- **Salad Dressing.** Scrape off the excess with a dull knife. Wash the item in heavy-duty detergent, using water as hot as is safe for the fabric.
- **Salt.** Remove salt marks from shoes and leather garments by wiping them with a solution of 1 part vinegar and 3 parts water.
- **Scorch Marks.** If the fabric is thick and fuzzy, brush it to remove charring first. Pretreat the area with heavy-duty liquid detergent, and wash the item with regular detergent. If stains persist wash the item again with regular laundry detergent and all-fabric bleach.
- **Self-Tanning Lotion.** Dab the stain with hydrogen peroxide and then launder as usual.
- **Shoe Polish.** Spray or dab the stains with dry-cleaning solvent. Then rub them with heavy-duty liquid detergent and launder as usual.
- **Smoke Damage.** Shake off soot outdoors. Launder using a heavy-duty phosphate-based detergent or heavy-duty liquid detergent. Add 1 cup water conditioner and ½ cup all-fabric bleach to the wash cycle. Use the water setting recommended for the fabric. Allow to air dry. Inspect the garment and repeat if necessary.

- **Soft Drinks.** Launder as usual. Don't use bar soap to try to remove the stain.
- **Soy Sauce.** If possible, don't let the stain dry. Blot the stain with a towel. Use a pretreatment and launder in cool water. If stains remain use an enzyme product to help break down the sauce and re-launder. For aged, set-in stains, apply a glycerin solution and let set for 25 minutes and then treat as previously recommended.
- **Steak Sauce.** Saturate stain with laundry pre-treatment (aerosol-types work best for this type of stain). Wait 3 minutes. Launder immediately. If stain remains, soak in chlorine bleach or in oxygen bleach, whichever is safest for the fabric.

- **Tea.** Wash the item with laundry detergent.
- **Tempura Paint.** Dye stains are difficult to remove. Pretreat the stain with a heavy-duty liquid detergent and rinse thoroughly. If the stain is on white or colorfast material, soak the garment in a diluted powdered bleach and water mixture for about 15 minutes.

- **Urine.** Soak the stains in cold water. Wash as usual. For stains on mattresses sponge the area with a mixture of water and detergent. Rinse with a mixture of vinegar and water. Let air-dry. If odor remains, sprinkle with baking soda and let it stand 24 hours. Vacuum the residue.

- **Vegetable Oil.** Treat the stain with a petroleum-base solvent pretreatment spray. Wash the item with heavy-duty detergent in hot water.
- **Vomit.** Scrape off any solid matter. Soak stains in cold water. Launder as usual.

- **Water Spots.** Launder garments as usual. For dry-cleanable fabrics, consult a professional dry cleaner.
- **Wine.** Soak stains in cold water. Launder as usual.

# Clean It Green

**B**ring out the natural beauty of your home by using these environmentally friendly cleaning suggestions. In this chapter the experts at *Better Homes and Gardens®* magazine bring you:

- **Materials and supplies** to clean it green
- **Homemade cleaning solutions** for kitchens, bathrooms, windows, walls, and more
- **Natural ways** to get rid of pests
- **Clean-it-green gift ideas**

## Materials and Supplies

**TIP 564**

**Use Baking Soda** as an odor-removing agent. Place an opened box in your refrigerator and freezer to neutralize odors. You also can sprinkle about 1 tablespoon down drains monthly to keep them smelling fresh.

**TIP 565**

**Use Borax** for a great water softener. It also penetrates and lifts out dirt. You can use it as an abrasive cleaner if you mix it with water in paste form.

**TIP 566**

**Use Chlorine Bleach** with caution. Don't spill it on surfaces where you don't want bleaching to occur. Never use it in combination with ammonia, because the combination can result in toxic fumes.

**Use Rubbing Alcohol** to sterilize household surfaces and everyday items.

**Mild Detergents** are in the cleaning section of most stores. Check labels for sodium laurel sulfate or ammonium laurel sulfate to verify mildness.

**Use Muriatic Acid** to clean tile and concrete. It's caustic, so use care when storing or handling it. Add the acid to water, never water to acid, to remove rubber, mortar, and mastic from plaster and tile. After mixing use it immediately and discard any remaining solution. Don't use on bathroom or kitchen tile.

**Be Careful** with turpentine, a very flammable solvent extracted from pine oil. Wear gloves when handling this product and avoid inhaling fumes.

**Use Liquid Soap And Baking Soda** as a natural tub and tile cleaner. Sprinkle about 1 tablespoon of baking soda on a damp rag. Add a little liquid soap to the rag and rub the area you want to clean. Rinse well.

**Vinegar** works great on windows, without harming the environment. If you try vinegar on windows for the first time, though, it may leave streaks. That's because commercial cleaners leave a very fine wax residue that vinegar can't remove. Add a dash of liquid detergent for the best results.

# Kitchen and Bathroom Cleaners

**Make Liquid Tub And Tile Cleaner** by mixing ½ cup ammonia, ½ cup white vinegar, ¼ cup baking soda, and 1 teaspoon borax. Put the mixture in a squeeze-top container. Shake before use. Scrub surfaces with a brush or sponge.

**Make Disinfectant** by mixing ¼ cup liquid bleach, ¼ cup lemon juice, and 3 cups water. Use it on tubs, showers, sinks, and other bathroom surfaces. Let it sit for 5 minutes after application. Rinse thoroughly.

**Make Lemon Countertop Cleaner** by mixing 1 cup liquid soap blend (see below), ¼ cup fresh-squeezed lemon juice, ¼ eyedropper tea-tree extract, and 6 cups warm water. Place solution in a plastic spray bottle, spray on, and wipe off. Store in a cool dark place and out of the reach of children. Shelf life: 4-6 months.

*(Liquid Soap Blend:* Mix ¼ cup glycerin soap flakes with ¾ cup boiling water until dissolved. If the soap hardens over time, simply reheat and add water until the mixture attains its original consistency. Shelf life: 4-6 months.)

**Make A Fresh-Smelling Disinfectant** by mixing ½ cup borax with 1 gallon hot water. Add a few sprigs of fresh thyme, rosemary, or lavender and allow to steep 10 minutes. Strain and cool before using. Essential fragrant oils work well, too, instead of fresh herbs. Store in a plastic spray bottle.

# Q.◆How can I clean mineral deposits on faucets?

# A.◆ **Rub Vinegar** onto the brownish stain that forms where a faucet drips or the water drains away. If the stain persists put paper towels soaked in vinegar on the stain and let them sit overnight.

# Flawless Windows, Walls, Ceilings, and Floors

**Make Homemade Window Cleaner** by mixing 1 cup white vinegar with 2 tablespoons rubbing alcohol to remove stubborn streaks from windows. Shelf life: 6-9 months.

**Make a Homemade Cleaning Solution** for walls by mixing 2 tablespoons ammonia or vinegar and 1 quart warm water. To remove heavy-duty dirt, mix 1 cup ammonia, ½ cup vinegar, and ¼ cup baking soda in 1 gallon warm water. First test the cleaning solution on an inconspicuous area to make sure it stays colorfast.

**Make Nail-Hole Filler** by mixing together 3 parts baking soda and 1 part white household glue. Mix and use immediately to fill small nail holes prior to painting. **Note:** As the mixture dries, it may shrink. You may have to fill it a second time just to make sure the wood is ready for painting.

**For Paint Remover** for glass, mix equal amounts of water and ammonia. Saturate the paint on windows. Be careful not to get the solution on the wood trim. Let it sit for 3-4 minutes and then peel off the paint with a razor blade.

**Clean Painted Walls** and washable wallpaper by mixing 1 gallon water with 1 cup apple cider vinegar. Wipe down the walls, doing a small section at a time. Shelf life: 6 months.

**Make A Multipurpose Cleaner** by mixing 1 gallon water, 1½ cups baking soda, ½ cup vinegar, and 3 tablespoons alcohol. This solution works well for cleaning paintbrushes and tools.

**Make A Carpet Freshener** by mixing 1 cup baking soda with ½ cup crushed lavender flowers. Mix well. Sprinkle on carpets liberally. Let sit for 30 minutes and then vacuum.

**Make Wood Floor Polish** by mixing 1 tablespoon beeswax in 2 cups mineral oil. Heat in a double boiler to melt the wax and blend the mixture. Apply the cooled solution to wood floors with a soft cloth.

**Make Carpet Revitalizer** by mixing 1 cup white vinegar and 2½ cups warm water. Spray a fine mist of the mixture on the carpet. Then scrub lightly with a brush. Let dry. Sift 1½ cups baking soda, 2 tablespoons cornstarch, and 3 drops vanilla essential oil together with a hand sifter, sprinkle it over dry carpet, and let sit for 2 hours. Vacuum. Shelf life: 2 weeks.

# Caring for Fine Furniture and Floors

**Tea Works Best** on wood floors. Brew two tea bags in 1 quart of boiling water and let the solution cool to room temperature. Mop the floor with the solution. The best part is: You don't have to rinse.

**Make Wood Cleaner** by combining ½ cup canola oil, ¼ cup liquid soap blend and ¼ cup water. Shake well before using. Apply with a soft cloth and buff to a shine.

# Q.◆ How should I handle alcohol spills on wood furniture?

# A.◆ Wipe Them Up Immediately, and rub the area with your hand. The oil in your hand restores some of that taken out of the wood by the alcohol.

**Remove Stains** from plastic laminate by rubbing them with a damp cloth dipped in baking soda.

**Remove Greasy Marks** from antique furniture with a chamois cloth soaked in a mixture of 1 tablespoon vinegar and 1 cup water. Wring out the chamois, wipe the surface, and dry completely with a soft cloth.

**Remove Stains** from upholstery by dabbing up spills right away. This prevents stains from setting.

### Make Your Own Dust Cloths

You can make your own treated dust cloths—super for furniture care—by following these directions:

1. **Mix a Solution** of 1 cup warm water, 1 tablespoon boiled linseed oil, ½ teaspoon dish soap, and ½ teaspoon ammonia.

2. **Soak the Cloths** in the solution and allow them to dry at room temperature. Store them in a sealed container until needed.

**TIP 591**

**Keep Wood Furniture** out of sunlight, as it will dry out the furniture's surface.

# Get Rid of Pests

Don't let those pesky pests get the best of you. Here are a few hints to help you manage them:

**TIP 592**

**Deter Ants** by sprinkling a few crumbled bay leaves on windowsills. To keep ants from invading your sugar and flour canisters, place several bay leaves inside.

**Kill Ants** with a mixture of 1 part borax with 1 part powdered sugar. Scatter it over a piece of stone or wood near the entrance to the nest. The ants are attracted by the sugar and poisoned by borax, which won't harm humans or animals.

**Discourage Mice.** Hang sprigs of mint in your kitchen cabinets or place them on shelves. Rub the plants often to release their scent.

## Experts' Advice

### Get Rid of Roaches

The most primitive of all winged insects, the roach hasn't changed in 300 million years. The good news is you can get rid of them by following these suggestions:

- **Keep Your Home Dry.** Roaches need water daily to survive. Fix leaky faucets, clean up dampness with towels, and don't leave water in sinks or tubs.

- **Clean Kitchen Surfaces,** such as countertops and shelves. (Roaches are attracted to areas where other roaches have been.)

- **Use A Home Recipe** to get rid of roaches. Stir together equal amounts of baking soda and powdered sugar. Leave the mixture in a shallow bowl where you have seen the roaches.

**Capture Spiders** by inverting a glass over them and sliding a piece of stiff paper under the glass. After trapping spiders, carry them outside.

**Keep Flies Out** by filling resealable sandwich bags with water, zipping them shut, and taping them to the outside of the door. The water bags will repel flies. Inside, use old-fashioned fly swatters instead of spray insecticides.

**Trap Earwigs** by rolling up newspaper, dampening it, and placing it outside near exterior doors.

**Eliminate Pet Carpet Odors.** Mix 1 cup vinegar, 1/2 cup baking soda, and 4 cups water. Scrub the carpet well. Allow it to dry and then vacuum. For additional scent, mix in 1 teaspoon vanilla or pineapple essential oil.

**Make Litter Box Deodorizer** by mixing 1 teaspoon baking soda into kitty litter. Measure the baking soda carefully. Too much may deter your cat from using the box.

**Bathe Pets** safely with water and castile soap. Make a tea using 1/3 cup fresh rosemary in 1 cup water. Strain. Scrub your dog with the castile soap and rinse the fur with the tea. This will deter fleas and give your dog's coat a healthy shine.

**Q.** How can I get rid of pet odor on hardwood floors?

**A.** **Mix equal amounts** of water and white vinegar. Wipe the mixture on the wood floor and let sit for up to 1 hour. Rinse and mop. **Note:** If your floors are wax-finished, vinegar will remove some of the wax.

**Make A Herbal Rinse** for pets. Add ½ cup fresh or dried rosemary to 1 quart boiling water. Let the mixture steep for 20 minutes. Strain the solution and let it cool. Sponge it on your pet's coat and massage it into the skin. Allow your pet's coat to air-dry or you'll remove the rosemary scent.

**Make Pet Disinfectant** by mixing ½ cup white vinegar and ¼ cup rubbing alcohol. Put the mixture in a spray bottle. Fill the rest of the bottle with water. Use this solution to clean in and around the pet food dishes. The area will stay clean and nontoxic to the animals.

**Control Fleas** in pet beds by cutting a purchased flea collar into 4–6 pieces. Place the pieces under the pet's bed or cushion.

**Repel Fleas** on your pet by mixing garlic into pet food. The odor will permeate the skin and act as a flea repellent. Or slice a lemon and place the pieces in boiling water. Let it cool. Pour the solution into a spray bottle, and spray on your pet 2-3 times weekly to deter fleas.

**Have Flea-Free Carpets.** To get rid of fleas on carpeting, sprinkle a light layer of borax on carpets and let it sit for 1 hour. Vacuum thoroughly. The borax will kill fleas and their eggs.

**Eliminate Pet-Bed Odors** with baking soda. It's nontoxic and safe to use around children and pets. Just sprinkle baking soda on the pet bed and the area around it. Let it sit 15 minutes. Then vacuum the pet bed.

**Vacuum Pet Hair** on furniture and carpeting easily. First, mix 1½ cups water with ½ cup fabric softener. Spray this solution on the furniture and carpet, wait 3 hours, and vacuum. The hair should vacuum up easily.

**Banish Rainy-Day** pet odors. Wipe your pet down with a new dryer sheet and make him or her smell springtime fresh in a matter of minutes.

**Remove Skunk Smell** from pets. Mix 1 part organic apple cider and 2 parts water. Bathe and rinse your pet thoroughly with this mixture. **Note:** Avoid getting the mixture in your pet's eyes because it will sting.

# Creative Gift Giving

Do you know someone who has just moved into a condo, house, or apartment? Or who has just added a pet to the family? One of these practical gifts may be the perfect housewarming present:

**TIP 610**

### Handyman's Heaven
- Plastic garbage pail in a brilliant color
- Multipurpose Cleaner–tip #582, page 162
- Concrete Cleaner–tip #645, page 181
- Decorative rags
- Homemade Hole Filler–tip #579, page 162
- Colored putty in a variety of colors
- Putty knife
- Squeegee

## Q.♦ When I wash my dog's blankets, hair gets in my washer and on my clothes. Help!

## A.♦ Use A Lint Brush to go over the blankets before washing. Discard any pet hair. Double-rinse the blankets and wipe out the inside of the washer with a dampened paper towel. If you put the blankets in the dryer, clean out the dryer lint trap immediately after you're done.

# Q. How can I find a cleaning service that cleans green and uses safe products?

# A. **Look In The Yellow Pages** of your local phone book and do a search on the Internet. Some national services will provide all-natural and nonallergenic cleaners if you just ask. Find out if they charge more to use these products.

**Housewarming Gift**
- This book
- Wood Floor Polish–tip #584, page 162
- Carpet Revitalizer–tip #585, page 162
- Homemade Hole Filler–tip #579, page 162
- Sponges
- Feather duster
- Houseplant polish
- Decorative mug filled with tea bags or coffee
- A useful basket to hold all of the above supplies

**New Pet**
- Dog leash
- Puppy or cat toy
- Shampoo
- Flea & tick repellant
- Herbal Rinse–tip #602, page 168
- Homemade Disinfectant–tip #603, page 168

# Appealing Attics, Basements, and Garages

 ttics, basements, and garages pose special cleaning challenges. They get dirtier than the rest of the house, yet they're cleaned less often. So dirt and dust buildup can be tough to clean.

These spots also require organization before you get to the actual cleaning. In this chapter you'll find a few ideas from the experts at *Better Homes and Gardens®* magazine to help you tidy up these spaces, such as the best ways to:

- **Clean concrete** walls and floors
- **Keep stored items dry** and mildew-free
- **Maintain windows** and floors
- **Protect these areas** from insects
- **Storage solutions** using proper containers

**Use Clear Plastic Bins** rather than cardboard boxes for storage. Cardboard boxes can absorb moisture from concrete walls and floors. Mildew may form on the boxes and the items inside. Plastic bins won't take on moisture, and you can see through them to recognize the contents stored.

**Avoid Stacking Boxes** or tubs on top of each other because you'll have to remove the top ones to reach the bottom ones.

**Store Holiday Ornaments** in empty liquor boxes. Each compartment will hold several layers of ornaments wrapped in tissue paper to keep them scratch-free.

**For Stale, Musty Odors,** use charcoal to fill a net vegetable bag, such as the kind onions come in, and hang one in each corner. The charcoal will soak up musty odors for some time.

**Remove Mold And Mildew Odors** by placing 1 cup white vinegar in opposite corners of a room (on the floor, under a table, or behind a piece of furniture) for 24 hours.

**Use Caution With Moth Balls.** They contain naphthalene, a poison when it's inhaled. Symptoms include headache, nausea, vomiting, shortness of breath, coughing, and burning eyes.

**Prevent Termites** in attics, basements, and garages by repairing leaky irrigation valves, spigots, or watering lines. Don't keep firewood in the garage, crawlspace, or house. Remove leaves near your home. Don't plant fence posts and porch pillars in the ground; support them with concrete footing. Make sure water drains away from your home. Check into professional termite treatments if you suspect your home is infested.

**Crickets.** Store boxes off floors and keep them tightly sealed. Fix leaky irrigation and drainage around the house. Seal openings leading into your home where crickets can live and mate.

**Scorpions.** Remove piles of lumber, trash, old boxes, and old clothes. Remove clutter from attics, basements, and garages so scorpions don't have a place to hide. Check cracks, crevices, and the foundation to control their entry into your home.

**Wasps And Bees** often build nests in attic walls. It's safest to call a professional pest control service to get rid of these.

## Experts' Advice

### Prevent Mold and Mildew in a Seasonally Vacant Home by:

1. **Setting The Thermostat at 85°** and making sure the thermostat fan switch is on "auto." Your central air conditioner will be able to control humidity more effectively.

2. **Leaving Interior And Closet Doors Open** so every room is properly ventilated.

3. **Checking The Air-Conditioner Filter** and installing a new one regularly. High-performance pleated filters are worth the money.

4. **Adjusting The Humidistat** if you have one. Placed on the proper setting, it will help control humidity. (**Note:** A humidistat is not always recommended by air conditioning contractors. Any misuse or incorrect settings can cause high electric bills.)

# Attacking the Attic

The best thing about cleaning the attic is the time you can spend reminiscing while you're cleaning. Old jeans, a T-shirt worthy of dirt, and a bandanna on your head are the only prerequisites for starting the job. A few hours a day will allow you to go through boxes at a leisurely pace. Or block out 3-4 hours on the weekend to get it done all at once.

**Dust** starting high and work your way down when dusting the attic. Always clean cobwebs from the bottom up to prevent them from splattering.

**Prevent Dampness** and mold by cleaning filters on humidifiers, dehumidifiers, air purifiers, and air-conditioners regularly. Ventilate the attic and basement as often as possible to keep storage items dry and free from a musty smell.

**Don't Vacuum Or Sweep** the attic (or any other area) if you think there might be rodents there. Some diseases carried by rodents are commonly contracted by breathing airborne particles. Instead, use damp mops and cloths where appropriate.

**Use A Dust Mop** or broom covered with a cloth to dust the rafters, ceiling, walls, and floors. Change or shake the cloth frequently.

**Dust Attic Floors** with a cloth-covered broom. Follow with a wet cleaning of clear water on wood floors. Wipe them dry fast.

**Ventilate The Attic** and crawl spaces to prevent moisture buildup. Relative humidity levels should be kept below 50 percent to prevent water condensation, which can breed bacteria.

**Mark Boxes** with the date that you go through them when you clean. Then check them again in another year. If you haven't used anything from the box in 2 years, consider donating them to a local charity.

**Beware Of Black Mold.** Check relative humidity levels in the attic to make sure that the moisture level is below 55 percent. Otherwise, you could find yourself battling black mold. Signs are:

- A musty odor on walls or floors
- Water-damaged or discolored walls

**If You're Cleaning** the attic because you're getting ready to sell your home, you're on the right track. Buyers always look in the attic to check out the space. Make sure there's adequate lighting, paint the walls if needed, and organize and stack boxes neatly.

**Store Luggage** in the attic. This way pieces will be clean and safe for their next use. Put a fresh dryer sheet in each piece of luggage to keep interiors smelling clean. Or fill them with neatly folded, out-of-season clothes.

**Store Holiday Decorations** by organizing them first into groups: lights, ornaments, wreaths, etc.

**TIP 634**

**Store Holiday Lights** without tangling them using cardboard or poster board. Cut a square out of cardboard or poster board. Then cut an opening in one side of the square and thread the lights through it. Keep wrapping the string of lights around the piece of cardboard, through the opening.

## Experts' Advice

### Organizing Attic Space

1. **Sort And Fill Boxes.** Begin by gathering sturdy boxes or "see-through" tubs. Sort through old boxes and piles of things, fill the new containers, and mark them clearly. You may want to start with a few extra boxes marked "trash," "donations," or "friends or family." Then put items in their respective containers as you go.

2. **Use The "1-Year Rule."** Mark one container "1-Year." Fill it with contents that you're not sure you want to give up. Then mark the date on the box and check it out in a year. By then you might be able to move those contents to "trash" or "donations" boxes.

3. **Clean First,** then store. If you plan to put clothes in the attic, have them dry-cleaned first. Storing them in dry-cleaning bags may cause discoloration.

4. **Deal With Nostalgia.** Items of sentimentality often work against your need to cut clutter. Take pictures of nostalgic items and then get rid of the items. The photos will bring back memories without the items actually taking up needed space.

# Battling Basement Blues

The basement sometimes becomes the dumping ground for anything that you don't use on a regular basis, such as Grandma's silver tea set, graduation photos, memorabilia, and that beautiful christening gown worn decades ago. What should you keep and what should you discard? And along the way, how do you keep it all clean? Well, the *Better Homes and Gardens*® magazine experts have come together to help you keep things clean, mold-free, and usable for many years to come.

**Don't Store Furniture** or electronics in the basement, because it can be damp. If you must store these items there, get a dehumidifier to take the moisture out of the air and put the items on pallets so they aren't sitting directly on the floor.

**Check For Moisture** in a basement by taping a 1-foot square piece of aluminum foil to the wall with duct tape. After a few days check the foil for moisture on both sides. If there is moisture on the side facing the wall, use a masonry sealer to waterproof the wall. If the foil side facing the room is wet, use a dehumidifier to circulate air and reduce condensation.

**Clean Up Water Damage.** To remove mildew or to clean basement floors after water damage, add 4 ounces sodium carbonate to 1 gallon hot water. Scrub the surface, let sit for 30 minutes, and then rinse with clear water.

**To Keep Your Basement Dry,** slope the ground by your foundation away from your house. This prevents water from gathering near the walls of the foundation.

**Clean Basement** window wells seasonally, and caulk around them if needed. This keeps water from building up and seeping in.

**Use Folding Screens** to hide stacked boxes in the corner of your basement.

**Q.** The previous owners of my home had dogs in the basement, and I think the odor from them has seeped into the concrete floor. Is that possible, and how can I get rid of the smell?

**A.** **Concrete is porous** and absorbent, so it's possible for the odor to have soaked into the floor. Use an enzyme cleaner on organic stains like urine. Treat the concrete floor with an enzyme cleaner, let it sit 20 minutes, and then rinse well. Vacuum the floor with a wet vacuum. Allow it to dry. If the odor remains repeat the process. Once the odor is gone, seal the concrete floor.

**TIP 641**

**Check For Safety.** Make sure paints and other flammable liquids are stored away from the hot water heater and furnace. This will prevent potentially hazardous fires.

## Experts' Advice

### How to Keep Basements Dry

- **Grade The Foundation** outside so that it slopes away from the house. The yard should be graded to direct water toward a drainage area.
- **Clear Gutters** of obstructions to direct water away from the house through the downspouts.
- **Caulk** around basement windows and doors.
- **Use Waterproof Paint** on the basement walls to help keep everything mold- and mildew-free.
- **Set Up A Dehumidifier** in the basement to keep relative humidity levels between 30%-50%.
- **Install A Sump Pump** with an automatic switch to keep water from backing up.
- **Install A Water Sensor.** It's an inexpensive backup for your sump pump–it will let you know if the basement surface gets wet.

**TIP 642**

**Keep Bulk Storage Items** in airtight containers near the entrance of the basement so that they will be dry and easily accessible.

**TIP 643**

**Consider Area Rugs** instead of carpeting for your basement. Unlike carpeting, area rugs can be removed for washing, repair, or replacement.

# Organizing Your Garage

The garage can get pretty dirty throughout every season because of the outside elements, yard maintenance equipment, bikes, and cars. Spruce things up at least annually, if not twice a year, to keep dirt from gathering and coming into the house. For garages, the experts at *Better Homes and Gardens*® magazine have compiled cleaning tips to keep this area dirt- and dust-free.

**Clean Unpainted Concrete** with a mixture of 4-6 tablespoons powdered laundry detergent or muriatic acid in 1 gallon hot water. These surfaces require special paints and sealers when you're done cleaning.

**Use Kitty Litter** or sawdust to soak up spills in the garage. Sprinkle the litter or sawdust on the spill and allow it to soak up the moisture. Then sweep up the litter and dispose of it. The spill will be gone too.

**Store Long-Handled Tools** handle side up in an old golf bag or in a large garbage can with wheels. That way you can wheel them around the yard as you're working and see the tool you need without removing several items.

**Keep Tools Clean** and rust-free by sticking them into a bucket of sand to store them when not in use. Cat litter works equally well.

**Deposit Hazardous Waste** products at a hazardous-waste site. Check with the local sanitation department for the location of the site and dates and times they accept these kinds of products.

**Wash Garage Windows** with a mixture of 3 tablespoons rubbing alcohol or vinegar, 1 tablespoon household ammonia, and 1 quart warm water. To save money polish windows with crumpled old newspapers instead of paper towels. **Note:** Don't use this cleaner on plastic glazing, because it will ruin the glaze.

**Clean Lawnmower Blades** before you mow by spraying them each time with nonstick cooking spray. They'll be easier to clean up and won't bring shards of grass into the garage.

**Hang Tools on a Pegboard** to keep them organized and close at hand.

**Store Seasonal Small Appliances** and decorations on shelves clearly marked so they're easily accessible.

**Store Loose Items,** such as garden or yard tools, in a box or bin to avoid clutter and injury. Use either a see-through plastic container, or label the box with contents, and date.

**Prevent Oil** from soaking into concrete floors by covering the floors with absorbent floor mats, available at most home improvement and discount stores. Some brands come in rolls you can cut to fit the surface area.

**Clean Oil From Garage Floors** by putting several layers of newspaper over the oil spot. Soak the paper with water, then allow it to dry. This will absorb much of the oil. If stains remain scrub with mineral oil or kerosene and wash with dishwashing detergent and warm water.

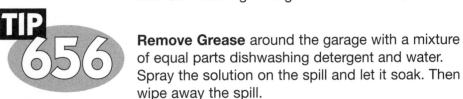

**Remove Grease** around the garage with a mixture of equal parts dishwashing detergent and water. Spray the solution on the spill and let it soak. Then wipe away the spill.

**Don't Pour Oil Paint,** paint thinners, or abrasive cleaners down garage drains. They may clog or damage them.

**Don't Wear** loose clothing or dangling jewelry when working with your car or tools in the garage, because these items can get caught in machinery.

# Help! I Need Somebody . . .

Cleaning the house all by yourself isn't fun. If you think getting your family to help you clean is the impossible dream, try some of the techniques below. When you add the rest of the family to the cleaning mix, you can have the recipe for fun just waiting to happen. Here are a few ideas from the experts at *Better Homes and Gardens®* magazine to get family members to help and stay motivated.

## Choose Age-Appropriate Chores

Be realistic about the cleaning chores your kids can do. It will help them be successful and develop a sense of pride in their accomplishments–not to mention all the help it gives you.

**Toddlers Ages 2–3 Can:**
• Pick up toys and return them to the toy box.
• Put books back on the shelves.
• Take dirty clothes to the laundry.
• Put socks on their hands and dust their furniture.

**Preschoolers Ages 4–5 Can:**
• Dust furniture.
• Set the dinner table.
• Clear the dinner table.
• Help put away groceries.

### Kids Ages 6–8 Can:
- Vacuum.
- Take out the trash.
- Take care of the family pet.
- Fold laundry.
- Put away laundry.

### Kids Ages 9–12 Can:
- Load dishes in the dishwasher.
- Wash and dry dishes by hand.
- Help make easy meals.
- Clean the bathroom.
- Do yard work such as raking leaves and pruning small bushes.

### Teens Ages 13–17 Can:
- Help with the laundry.
- Clean windows.
- Clean appliances in the kitchen.
- Vacuum most of the house.
- Prepare meals.
- Shop for groceries.

**Q.** How can I make hectic mornings easier on myself and my family?

**A. Set The Breakfast Table** the night before, after you clean up from dinner. It'll save you time in the morning.

## Experts' Advice

# How to Get Your Family to Help

- **Turn On The Tunes.** Have family members select music to accompany them as they clean. Propose a competition. The person to pick up the most dirty laundry gets to play music first for a set time period. Then set up the next competition with a different task involved, such as dusting the living room. Everyone will eventually get to hear his or her favorites, and the time will fly by.

- **Work In Teams.** Set up teams to compete against each other by shooting dirty laundry into the clothes hamper and seeing who makes the most "baskets." Make sure prizes work well for everyone— like sandwich shop coupons for adults, phone cards for teens, or toy store gift certificates for children.

- **Set A Timer** to see who can dust a room the fastest or finish cleaning a bedroom closet first. Winners will delight in choosing an inexpensive prize such as a large chocolate bar, a scented candle, cream-filled cupcakes, or a small toy.

- **Take Breaks.** Set up breaks between the cleaning chores so no one burns out before all tasks are finished. Bake or buy buttermilk brownies and set up a time to share brownies and milk to keep your workers going strong.

# Calling in the Pros

If your family is too busy or not willing to help you clean, you may want to try a cleaning service. Maybe you don't have time to do it all yourself. Maybe you can't clean because of a disability or allergies to cleaning products. Maybe you just need to free up your time to fit in more time with your family.

Whatever the reason, hiring a service doesn't need to be stressful. Follow these suggestions to take the guesswork out of questions you may have on finding a cleaning service:

- **Where to find help** when you're ready for it
- **What questions to ask** when you're interviewing a service
- **How to check** on the reputation of a cleaning service
- **Which day of the week** might work best for your family

# Finding the Best Service

When you're ready to hire a service, you don't have to take potluck from the phone book or neighborhood shopper publication. Don't feel you have to automatically hire the neighbor who has a cleaning business. Here are a few ways to find a good service:

**TIP 664**

**Call Cleaning Services** for information on what they clean and their various prices and plans (weekly, monthly, or semiweekly).

**Ask Your Friends,** relatives, and colleagues at work for their recommendations.

**Contact Local Real Estate Offices** and ask for recommendations. They usually have reliable professional cleaning services they suggest to their new homeowners and buyers.

**Send An E-Mail** to the "frequent contacts" on your e-mail address list asking for suggestions. The more options you have, the better the chance you might find a great cleaning service that's perfect for you.

**Hire High School Kids.** They're usually eager to make money and willing to learn how you like things done. And they may cost less than a professional service. You could ask a local school guidance office for recommendations.

**Once You've Decided** on a service or professional, contact the Better Business Bureau to check on their reputation.

**Be Home** during your first cleaning with a professional service if possible. You'll be able to give any special instructions in person, and show them you pay attention to details.

# TIP 671
## Questions to Ask a Cleaning Service

Determining your housecleaning needs is just the first step when it comes to finding a good cleaning service. You'll need to interview the service and make sure it's a good fit for you and your family. Here are a few questions to ask:

❑ **What cleaning services are provided?** You might want to make your wish list first and then make sure a service comes close to meeting all your needs.

❑ **How do they price** their services, and what will be the final cost?

❑ **Are there extra costs** for special tasks, such as cleaning the oven?

❑ **What time and day** will they arrive? How do they handle scheduling problems or if your cleaning day happens to be a holiday? (Do they cancel for that week, or do they try to reschedule?)

❑ **Are there discounts** for more frequent service, such as weekly cleanings versus monthly ones? How would they like payment?

❑ **Do they stay a set time** period or leave when the cleaning is done?

❑ **Will it be the same team** every time, or do they rotate teams?

❑ **Do they need your keys** to get access to your home?

❑ **Are they bonded and insured** in case of theft or breakage?

❑ **Are you liable for workers' compensation** if they are hurt while cleaning your home?

❑ **What will the cleaners expect** you to do before they arrive?

❑ **What supplies and equipment** will you provide, and what will the cleaners provide?